# the Prairie
# Remembers

Janice Brozik Cerney

Library of Congress Control Number: 2002092743

ISBN: 1-57579-246-X

Cover photo of a breaking plow taken at the Oscar
Micheaux Homestead Site near Gregory, South Dakota.

Back cover photo taken at Barbara Hataj's
Homestead Site. Vincent, Jr. standing in the background.

*Printed in the United States of America*
PINE HILL PRESS
4000 West 57th Street
Sioux Falls, S.D. 57106

# Preface

Perhaps this story began when my parents took me to the Grim place near the river breaks to check cattle. My dad farmed 160 acres ten miles north of Gregory, but in the spring we would drive the cattle ten miles north to pasture for the summer on 280 acres of grazing land that bordered the holdings of his parents. A trip to the Grim place was always an adventure for me, for there was always something interesting and new at the top of the hill, at the bottom of the next ravine or around the next bend of the creek. Nestled in the trees and shrubs of a creek bottom stood a sod house built by the homesteader Grim. With my dad, I remember exploring the thick sod walls papered with newspaper and the deep-set windows. The isolation of it all held a certain mystical quality-to imagine that only a few years before someone had lived in a dwelling cut from native sod.

I have always been enamored by the secret stories locked within the landscape of crumbling riverbanks, lofty hills, wide plains, and meandering valleys. To me these hidden stories begged to be told. Using my grandparents and their extended families, I have brought them back to these pages to tell one such tale of immigrating to America, homesteading in Dakota, and enduring the years of the Dust Bowl.

Although my great grandparents and my grandfather died before I was born, and I never knew my great uncles and aunts, I used what information I had to shape their characters and events into a fictional story following a historical timeline.

My grandmother Marie lived until I was fifteen years old. She only spoke Bohemian so we really didn't communicate the way I would have liked, although she taught me Bohemian words, mostly nouns. I could ask for a cup of coffee and a piece of bread if I wanted, but I was always too shy. However, I enjoyed her soups, the peppermint candy she kept in her cupboard, and the practical Christmas gifts she gave to me.

No doubt there will be inaccuracies regarding some events, time sequence and my interpretation of thoughts and characters, but that is not as important as what my grandparents accomplished. These brave pioneers unknowingly contributed in building a nation by settling the West and in return left a part of themselves, blending the culture of their homeland into the American way of life, and leaving a legacy for future generations.

This is their story, but it could be the saga of many a homesteader whose zest for life and courageous spirit have shone through for over a hundred years of remembering.

# Acknowledgements

I would like to take this opportunity to thank the many people who have contributed to this book. I offer a special thanks to my cousins, aunt, immediate family, and to friends of the family. Thanks to Bud and Marie who took the time to take me to the claim sites during the blistering heat of August. I appreciate the handed down stories you all shared with me. Thanks Bob for your untiring search for old photographs. Thank you to those who encouraged me and helped critique my work. Without your assistance, this story would not have been told.

# Table of Contents

*To my father who loved the land*
*To my mother who still likes to tell the stories*
*Of the "Good Ole Days"*

*Frank and Marie, 1902.*

*Chapter One*

# Saying Goodbye

The tall prairie grasses ripple in the never-ending prairie wind. In the distance a team and wagon heads north, a mere speck in the vast landscape of prairie and sky. Bright sunshine glistens on the ocean of grass warming the earth with each ray. The prairie wind whispers its song of primeval ages, telling its stories of the past. A man and a woman sit perched on a wagon seat lost in their own thoughts as they travel to their homestead in the northeastern corner of Gregory county unaware that their lives are but a fleeting moment in time. Unknown to them, they are making history by settling the land and making a way for their descendants.

It has been nearly two days since they left the farm in Spencer, Nebraska. The weather has been cool, the ride jostling and monotonous, but Frank promises they are about there. Marie (MAR-yeh) looks forward to an already established house on the claim, even if it is a soddy. Out of habit, she peers over her shoulder to see if Frank's brother Vaclav (VAHT-slav) and his family are still following behind in a hayrack with their possessions using the only transportation they have available. Marie glances back in the wagon to her seven month old baby nestled on feather ticks between a wicker and steamer trunk. Her eyes linger on the brown reeds of the wicker trunk carrying her thoughts back almost five years earlier to a dimly lit cottage in Tojice, Bohemia.

There, within the circle of family, quiet voices murmur fears, hopes, and aspirations. Marie sits anxiously across the table from Frank as he and his parents, sisters and brothers make decisions that will affect the rest of their lives as well as generations to come. Should they leave their homeland and migrate across an ocean of unknown possibilities? Frank's mother Barbara rereads a letter she received this morning from her daughter Teresa in Cleveland who immigrated earlier to America. The family listens intent on every word. The encouraging letter says, "The newspapers are full of work opportunities. Class does not bind people here. There's definitely hope for a better future." Barbara places the read letter with the pamphlets that paint a bright, rosy picture of America with its endless opportunities to lure the immigrants to America to settle the West. Each of the brothers studies the pamphlets over and over again.

"How do we know all this is true?" says Frank. "We have talked to some of our neighbors who have received letters that offer discouraging news of settling in America. Some say that life is hard. They are homesick and would like to come home but cannot afford the trip back."

"But why stay here?" argues Vaclav. "There is no future. Land is scarce and farm prices continue to fall. Brother Josef (YOO-sef) has found land in Nebraska to farm. So far, he seems to like it there."

"We all want to farm," another brother Mike hastens to add. "And how can we farm the small holdings father has?"

We need more land. The way it is now all the rich foreigners own our land. Debt and foreclosure are a constant threat."

"Besides, even if we gave up our dream of farming, work is hard to come by. The population is growing making jobs hard to find. Working for foreigners isn't my idea of a future," says Frank.

Marie gives Frank a quick glance. She too agrees with his statement.

The family continues their conversation discussing how they will pay for their passage to America. Adult passage aboard ship will cost the family about sixty-five to seventy American dollars per person, more money than they have for everyone to leave at the same time. In addition, immigration policy requires all incoming passengers to have money with them to pay for a railway ticket and enough cash to make a start in America. They will also have to give a destination point upon arrival to ensure that the masses of immigrants will not be a burden on America.

They also talk over the military obligation of eleven years of service in the German army fighting wars far from home. The brothers, bound to the mandatory service, need to obtain permission from the government or find a way to sever their commitment in order to leave. The family agrees that Albert, the youngest son, should leave soon before he becomes eligible for military service.

Even though leaving seems like the right decision, doubts nag at them, especially for the parents who have lived most of their lives in Bohemia. Generations of their ancestors lie buried in the village graveyard. Are they, the aging parents, too old to start a new life? But they remind one another of their daily lives, living like peasants with no choices or voice in their government. They remember the many injustices perpetrated by the Austrian Emperor and his government. Authorities flogged the women for gathering firewood and destroyed the traps and snares of the farmers so they could not catch wild game to eat or sell to the rich for money to buy a few necessities. They remember the church demanding allegiance and in the meantime taking their land as well as attempting to destroy their culture, their very identity.

"I want to go and see for myself if what they advertise in the newspapers and pamphlets is true. Teresa writes that there is work at the smelter plant in Cleveland," proposes Frank as he points to the letter. "I can live with her until I can get money to buy land and send money for passage. According to these pamphlets 160 acres of land is affordable in America."

After careful consideration of all the options, the brothers agree and make the decision that all of the brothers should go as soon as possible to America. The sisters will also emigrate but perhaps a little later.

With the conversation ended and the decision made, Frank and Marie leave the room and go outside to be alone. They continue the discussion between themselves and check on the animals living in the lower level of the cottage. Frank pushes the cows a few more beet leaves before he and Marie sit down, hand in hand, on a bench to gaze on the same stars that each would see every night even though they will be oceans apart, a small consolation for the time they would not be together. "I'll send for you as soon as I can, and we will start our life together," promises Frank.

Several months later in November of 1900 after tearful farewells and promises of frequent letters, Frank leaves on the crowded steam ship 'Prinz Regent Luitpold' from the German port of Bremen bound for America.

Months pass before Marie receives a letter from Cleveland. Frank assures her that he is all right. Work in the smelter plant is hard, but he is accumulating funds to buy land out West. He explains to her that all the good land has been taken in the East. The only land available now is in the West in such states as Minnesota, Iowa, Nebraska and the Dakotas. He goes on to say that there are many Bohemian people in Cleveland who have been arriving since 1849. He misses the family, but the community of his kinfolk helps ease his homesickness. "We get together, play music, and sing old songs," he writes.

Over the course of the year, Frank updates her on his progress. "I have found a place to rent in Nebraska near my brothers Albert and *Josef* as well as by some of our old friends in Bohemia who have filed on claims near Spencer. Soon you should be able to join me." She rereads his letters until the creases are worn and the ink has started to blur.

Other letters tell of his trip to Nebraska. "I took the train from Cleveland to Yankton, South Dakota, as far as the rails went. At Yankton I boarded a steamboat by the name of 'Castalia' making its run from Sioux City, Iowa, up river. The steamboat was a pretty sight resting on the water. I watched it come in, its stern paddle wheel churning the water and propelling it along, the two smoke stacks on the prow puffing smoke. It had two decks, the bottom deck filled with cargo and merchandise for the river towns. It returns down river with cattle and hogs to markets in the East. Too bad I'll miss that trip with the squealing pigs." Marie chuckles to herself. He really never did like pigs.

The letter continues. "A cabin with windows occupied part of the lower deck for passengers to get in out of the weather. I spent most of my time on the upper level so I could see the country. They call the river the Big Muddy, because it is always churning up dirt from floods and crumbling riverbanks. The captain, perched in his pilot's house, seemed to know what he was doing. Much to my relief, he steered us clear of all the snags and sand bars. I heard stories of several steamboats wrecking each year. I'm glad we weren't one of them." She turns the letter over, his writing scrunched on every available space to conserve paper. She, too, is glad he made the trip safely.

She eagerly reads on. "It took about a day to reach Iron Post Landing near Gross, Nebraska. I can't say I got tired of the scenery though. There's something new around every bend. A man told me that they use the white chalk from the river bluffs for building material. You can see evidence of this in the town where we landed. When we arrived at Iron Post Landing, marked with a square iron post, Albert and *Josef* were there to greet me. Like I said, there's a town at the landing, so we stopped for something to eat before we went to the place they are living to spend the night. The next day they took me to the place I rented between Gross and Spencer. This land is strange and will take some getting use to, although it does remind me some of Bohemia with its hills. There are few trees and the wind seems to blow continuously across the prairie, but it is so open and free. Tonight, as I write this letter, the wind sends such a mournful sound down the stovepipe. This will be temporary. Soon you will all join me."

Marie begins to formulate plans in her mind of her voyage to America. Then, she too, can see what this America is like. In her anticipation of the upcoming voyage, she decides to go shopping in the village with her mother for a trunk so she can start packing the few possessions she will take along. The hustle and bustle of the little village adds to her height of euphoria. She catches snatches of conversation along the way. Others, too, are concerned that the Industrial Revolution in Europe along with its prosperity has not reached their region. More and more homefolk talk of emigrating. The feeling of unrest permeates the air. Posters tacked up on walls advertise America. A returning emigrant sits on the street telling tales as well as answering questions about America to spellbound town folk.

"Mother, what do you think about this trunk?" Marie asks her as she examines it closely testing its durability.

Taking Marie aside, she whispers, "See if he will come down in price. I think it is too costly. You will need every cent for America."

"Yes, but he needs the money too. Times are bad here."

After agreeing on a price, Marie buys the lightweight wicker trunk from the local artisan. The size and lightness will be something she can handle, and it will hold her possessions that she will take to America. The youthful spring in her step and the firm determination on her face carry her home for one last time.

At last the long awaited day has arrived. She finally finishes packing the trunk. Each day she has added to the trunk, only to reconsider and take out what she has packed before. She finds it difficult to pack her life into a small trunk. Frank has warned her that baggage handlers are sometimes unscrupulous and that valuables should not be packed away. She carefully sews her favorite brooch into the lining of her petticoat and sews a money belt to hold her money for safekeeping. Frank's letters have also prepared her for what discomforts she will have to endure in the lower steerage of the ship. "The bunks are small and hard with only a light, thin mattress stuffed with straw," he writes. "Make sure to take along blankets to ward off the chilly sea air and add softness to the hard bunks."

The thought of Frank waiting for her in America gives her the final push of courage she needs to say good-bye to her mother, who will emigrate soon also, and to board the train that will take her and her future brother-in-law, Vaclav and sister-in-law, Barbara to the port of embarkation. Aboard the train, the familiar countryside glides past the window of the railroad car. Her beautiful country, with its tree covered mountains, languid flowing rivers, and green valleys, fades from sight. She takes a deep breath. She cannot turn back now.

Mile after mile of her old life retreats behind her. Finally, she catches sight of a large steamship looming on the oceanfront. The train slows and lurches to a halt. She steps off the train to breathe the salt air and to listen to sea gulls cry their faraway call of the sea. Waves splash against the shoreline as they line up to join the streams of emigrants waiting to board the ship. The steamship crew anxiously crowds as many emigrants as possible onto the ship. The line moves slowly as each one is stopped and questioned. Passengers must give information in the form of a manifest. This information, as well as a record of a physical exam before embarkation, will expedite the process once they arrive in America. Failure to do this might result in deportation at the shipping line's expense.

The ship's crew separates the men and women as they crowd into the steerage, the lowest level of the ship, to find a place for their belongings and secure a small space for themselves. Barbara, Vaclav's fiancée, and Marie stay close to one another as they make their way below deck.

"Over here," calls Marie. "This is as good a place as any."

"These bunks are so hard and small," remarks Barbara as she tests the firmness with her hand.

"Do you want the top or lower one?" Marie asks taking out her blanket from the trunk to cover the thin straw mattress.

"The top one will be fine. I suppose we shouldn't complain. It took months to travel across the ocean in dangerous wooden sailing vessels not too many years ago. We will have to put up with discomfort for only a few weeks now that we are sailing on a steamship."

"It's hard to catch a breath of air in here. Let's go out on deck and watch the shore as we sail away," suggests Marie as she drapes a shawl over her shoulder.

The women feel the gentle movement of the ship as it slowly edges out of the harbor. Salty sea air stings at already misty eyes as the coast recedes into the distance. They watch as the land, their only connection with their past, disappears from sight.

The calm seawaters ripple out from the prow of the ship. The smooth departure eases the turbulent emotions of those venturing forth to a new land with unknown certainty.

Today, the passengers move around freely enjoying calm seas, chatting with one another as to place of origin and destination. Later in the day, the women join Vaclav for the evening meal of thin porridge and dark bread served on long tables.

"I'm glad we packed away some cheese and fruit to add to our diet," remarks Marie as she pushes aside her empty bowl.

"There will be plenty to eat in America," assures Vaclav getting up from the table. "Now where is that cheese? This meager meal will not hold me for long."

The ship glides over the tranquil sea for several more days. During the night of the third day, the women awaken to a violent pitching motion. Marie tries to hold on to the bunk to prevent from being thrown to the floor. The sound of retching from seasick passengers sickens her already queasy stomach. Tempted to go out on deck to get fresh air, she remembers the warning about being thrown overboard by the pitching ship. She, as well as the other green-faced passengers, must endure their confinement for several more days. Spirits dampen along with the mist from the rumbling waves.

The sea calms once again. The passengers roam about and sun themselves on deck. "Have you heard there is a contagious disease on board?" worries Babara.

"That's one of my greatest fears," says Marie. "Anyone arriving in America unhealthy will be placed in confinement or even be deported. We must be careful not to catch anything."

"That won't be easy especially because of the crowded conditions. Trying to wash and keep clean is nearly impossible."

"It won't be long now," reflects Marie as she checks off another day on a piece of paper. A few days at best."

True to her word, several days later someone shouts, "Land!" The tired, bewildered passengers rush to the deck to glimpse the shoreline, their awaiting future. A mixture of emotions pervades. Excitement mingles with dread. They have heard the stories of the landing. At first, it was Castle Garden as the point of debarkation. Now, it is the recently built Ellis Island. Beware of swindlers and corrupt officials, others have warned. Stories are told, too, of rejected immigrants that had to return to their homeland due to recently enacted immigration laws requiring thorough inspection of emigrants upon arrival.

These thoughts nag at Marie as she and Barbara line up to fetch their bucket of water for washing. They try to do their best to make themselves presentable when they set foot on American soil. Carefully smoothing out the wrinkles of their best dresses, they wish they weren't so tired and apprehensive.

Several islands come into view as the ship eases into New York harbor. Tall buildings rise out of the horizon. A goddess holding a torch breaks through a thin haze. "Who is she?" some ask. The ship halts beside other ships waiting in the harbor filled with immigrants.

"We will have to wait here for awhile," explains Vaclav who recently rejoined them on deck. "When they have processed the immigrants already there on the island, they will send the ferry for us."

From afar, they study the red brick building of Renaissance style sprawled across Ellis Island with its towers, arched doorways and windows. Marie thinks it resembles some of the castles she left behind in Bohemia. They have been told that thousand of immigrants pass through its Golden Doors each day. What will they all find within its doors? Will it be acceptance or rejection?

Nervous tension quiets the passengers. Marie rehearses the answers to questions she will be asked by the inspectors. If the answers correspond to the manifest and the medical exam goes well, she should be on her way in a few hours. Will she be that lucky? What happens if the inspector misunderstands her answers?

After several hours of waiting a barge pulls along side of the ship to ferry the passengers to Ellis Island. Tired and hungry immigrants crowd onto the barge. After arriving at the island, the weary passengers leave the barge and are escorted under a long canopy leading to the baggage area. Marie leaves her trunk here while she goes through the processing. First, begins the questioning of the inspectors. A vaulted ceiling, in the massive room on the second floor of the great building, rises above iron railings partitioning off the large expanse where the inspectors stand ready to question the incoming arrivals. People from all parts of the world dressed in native costumes and speaking numerous languages fill this great room.

Beads of perspiration form on Marie's face. Her heart flutters with each beat. She is next in line to answer the inspector's questions.

"Full name," gruffs the inspector.

"Marie Hataj."

"Age."

"Twenty."

The questions continue for several more minutes, but they seem like hours to her. Questions completed and answered satisfactorily, she proceeds on to the medical exam. Being in good health she has little to fear, but she cannot be certain that she has picked up something contagious from the voyage. A doctor holds a tool that resembles a buttonhook. She dreads this ominous devise as he quickly lifts the eyelid looking for trachoma, a contagious incurable disease of the eye. The doctors look for other physical defects and check the scalp for favus, a highly contagious scalp disease. She notices that some passengers have chalk marks on their clothing denoting the particular condition the medical staff wants to investigate further. She completes the exam without any chalk marks.

Marie, Barbara, and Vaclav pass inspection. Officials direct them downstairs to exchange their foreign currency for American money and to purchase railway tickets to their destination. They buy their tickets and receive tags to be pinned to their clothing giving information as to their destination. Afterwards, the barge ferries them to the railway station. The grim line on their anxiety filled faces softens into relief. They have been accepted in America.

Aboard the train, Marie sinks down to the wooden seat of the railway car breathing a deep sigh of relief. The click clack of the railroad cars lulls her senses and eases her fears. One major obstacle of the trip has been overcome. Now she enjoys the prospects of building a new life. She closes her eyes and listens to the rhythm of the train coursing through the country on its steel track, bringing her closer and closer to Frank and her new home.

The railroads, in their ambition to settle the West for their own gain, not only push for settlement by advertising free land in pamphlets, newspapers, guide books, and on posters often distorting reality and embellishing the truth, but they also provide one way only transportation to the West on immigrant trains from the ports of entry on the East coast. The rates on these trains are often cheaper compared to the express trains of the day. Even at that Marie questions the implication of the bargain, crowded ninety to a car sitting on board seats which she makes more comfortable by padding it with her quilt. Sleeping in tiers of wooden cubicles, posing as sleeping cars amongst crying and fussing children, tests her patience. Although she finds the accommodations clean but trying at times, she does her best not to complain.

The train provides cooking facilities on board for the travelers to prepare their own food during the weeklong trip, but the food becomes tiresome with little variety. Occasionally, the train pulls into a lodging house especially built by the Union Pacific for the immigrant trains. Here, the travelers enjoy a good meal at a fair price and respite from the confinement of the cars.

The country changes as they travel farther west. The cities and towns become fewer and fewer, the land more sparsely settled. Hills stretch out to flat prairie devoid of trees. Claim shacks, hastily constructed of thin boards, lath, and tarpaper, and houses made of earth replace the impressive structures of the east. Their simplicity looks meager in the vastness of space. Frank wrote about sod houses and the sparseness of the region but seeing with her own eyes jars her into reality. Weariness from changing trains and the close quarters of the stuffy cars make her drowsy. Whatever lies ahead, she will deal with it.

"O'Neill, Nebraska," announces the conductor as the Chicago Northwestern comes rumbling to a halt. Marie jerks her head up from her catnap and eagerly peers through the grime covered windows out onto a bustling town, a trading center, and the end of the railroad line for many.

She steadies herself as she prepares to step off the train. Searching the crowd for Frank, she wonders if the year of separation has changed the way they feel about one another.

"There's Frank," Vaclav shouts as he points him out among the crowd.

Frank edges forward. Marie notices that he appears a little more robust and muscular in spite of his small five foot, six inch build. A new vitality plays around his teasing smile.

The year apart and the nervousness melt away like a spring thaw as they renew their commitment to one another. "So much to catch up on. Where does one begin?" Marie thinks to herself.

Frank proudly shows off his newly acquired Belgian team of workhorses as they climb into the wagon. Laughter and voices excited with news resonate in the crisp air. "I have rooms for us at the hotel," Frank breathlessly explains as he loads the trunks into the wagon. "If the weather permits, we will get an early start to Spencer in the morning."

A real bed! It's a pleasant image to the weary travelers that edges out memories of lodging facilities that weren't often satisfactory during their long trip. With the number of people trekking across the country, it is often difficult to find quality accommodations.

Upon arrival at the hotel, the men and women part company. Once in their room, Marie turns down the bedding checking for bed bugs or unclean linen. To her satisfaction, all appears well.

"I think I'll go and see about a tin tub," says Barbara. "It's been days since we have been able to clean up properly."

"A nice bath before supper sounds good to me, and we can also wash out some clothing," agrees Marie. "It might be some time before we have this much water available as well as a tub."

After settling into the rooms, the women join the men for supper in the hotel dining room. The aroma of roasted meat and potatoes steam up from large bowls and platters that fill the center of the long table spread with a red and white-checkered cloth. An odd assortment of travelers jabbering in various languages pass the food down the table nodding a friendly greeting to their newly acquired neighbors.

The two couples have much to talk about. First, they discuss news of back home, and then Frank updates them on the homestead.

"How long will it take to get there?" asks Marie as she sips her second cup of coffee.

"About two days," replies Frank. "The canvas cover over the wagon will provide shelter from the elements for us. If our luck holds, we won't run into any bad weather. None of you have seen a prairie blizzard. It's a sight to behold, but it is best seen from a snug house. We will spend the next night with some homesteaders along the way. In this country, the latch-string is always out for travelers far from home."

Marie suppresses an involuntary shudder as she stares out at the void of darkness. Indeed, this land will take some getting use to.

Luckily the sun shines bright and warm on the next morning. After a night of rest and a good breakfast of oven toasted bread and eggs, the couples bundle themselves up against the brisk air. Frank hitches up the team that he boarded for the night at the livery stable. The night stay has been costly for the meager income of the homesteader.

The eager horses maneuver the wagon down a well-worn trail north to Spencer. The sojourners in this strange land snatch glimpses of the countryside. Marie, now able to see the land up close, notices the sod structures she saw from the train. Smoke curls up from the odd looking huts. Geraniums blooming inside the houses press their faces to the glass panes of the deep-set windows. The petal-like blades of the windmills glint in the winter sun. Marie remarks to Frank about the number of windmills in the country. Frank responds by saying it is because of all the shallow wells in the area. An unusual coziness creeps into the winter prairie where every breath of life seems stilled. The country changes from flat land to hills, resembling pincushions, spiked with the narrow needle- blades of the soap weed covering every knoll. "They call this area the Sandhills," Frank informs them. "Just when you think that this is all there is to see, you drop down into a valley that is lush green in the spring. The cattlemen and the homesteaders are having quite a fight over who will occupy it."

The sameness of the chilled landscape begins to wear on the newcomers during the second day. "Our friends from Bohemia will have supper waiting for us. They live just a few miles out of Spencer. You and Barbara will stay with them for a few days until we are married," explains Frank.

Toward the end of the second day, the town of Spencer appears on the horizon. Now ten years old, it sprawls one hundred feet above the Ponca Valley below. Short and sparse trees dot the hillsides-more trees than anyone has seen for some time. The Missouri River borders the isolated town on the east, and the Sandhills border it to the south. The railroad due to arrive within the year will make the town more accessible. The couples arrive none too soon at their destination as the cold begins to penetrate their wraps. Familiar smells of favorite foods from the old country greet them as they enter the house of their old friends. Fresh baked *houska*, a braided holiday bread, and sauerkraut and dumplings with a hint of caraway entice the appetite of the weary travelers who have not enjoyed a traditional home cooked meal for some time.

Good food and good friends offer the best welcome to America yet. Well into the evening, Frank and Vaclav depart for the homestead. The women remain with their friends until wedding plans are made.

*Chapter Two*
# New Beginnings

Marie carefully folds a white linen handkerchief trimmed with artfully handcrafted Bohemian lace, a gift from her mother for her wedding day. She tucks it neatly in the belt of her best long sleeved dress and fastens the garnet brooch, an engagement present from Frank, on the neckline of her dress. She studies her reflection in the mirror while putting the final touches to her hair. Today, she does not place the crowning band of flowers in her hair, a traditional custom for unmarried girls in her homeland. The band removed during the wedding ceremony and replaced with a cap signifies the rite of passage of the bride to a married woman. Nor does she wear the bright, heavily embroidered dress. It's different in America. Frank won't be wearing his traditional garb with a hat embellished with flowers and clipped feathers, one for each of his former girlfriends. Frank, sitting in the kitchen waiting for her today, looks handsome in his three-piece suit and American tie.

After the double wedding ceremony of Frank and Marie and Vaclav and Barbara on January 9, 1902, in St. Mary's Catholic Church, a small frame building, children soon fol-

*St. Mary's Catholic Church, Spencer, Nebraska.*

low. A boy and a girl, Joe and Mary, are born to Barbara and Vaclav. Frank and Marie lose their first-born son at three months of age in this land often inhospitable to children. They bury him in a graveyard in Gross. Children, especially vulnerable to the lack of medical care, improper nutrition, and the severe environmental conditions, often leave the world early. But another son, Charley, and daughter, Anna, follow quickly. The comfort of being around relatives and neighbors from the Old Country helps with the adjustment in a foreign land. But the dream of owning their land has not become a reality.

In the spring of 1904, Frank rushes into the house with information. "The town is humming with news that President Theodore Roosevelt has issued a proclamation opening up part of the Rosebud Indian Reservation for set-tlement in South Dakota. They're using a lottery system to parcel out 160 acre plots to avoid the land rush confusions of the past. One of the registration points is Bonesteel, not too far from here. What do you think, Vac?"

Vaclav stirs cream into his coffee before he responds. "I think it is worth a try. There is no available land here."

"I think it's too risky," mutters Marie under her breath. "Gatherings such as this bring the gamblers and the crooks."

In spite of the women's protests, the brothers board the train in July for Bonesteel only to return within a few days filled with stories of lawlessness, riots, and no luck in the draw. "It's fortunate we came back with anything left in our pockets. There were pickpockets everywhere," admits Frank.

"One man we talked to was picked clean. It's a good thing he already had purchased his return railroad ticket," says the relieved Vaclav, glad to be home once again. "Well what could we expect? There were people everywhere hoping to get lucky and draw the winning numbers. Our chances were slim."

"Were you able to find a place to sleep with so many people milling around?" says Marie.

"We were able to rent a cot for twenty-five cents a night in a barracks type building. Although, I can't say I slept much. We took turns sleeping and standing in line at the registration office," says Frank. "Not that it did much good. If we wait, land will eventually come up for sale at a cheaper price. It may not be the choice land, but it will be land."

The men purposely leave out details of their two-day stay in Bonesteel, named the White City because of all the white tents pitched on any available piece of ground by the optimistic land seekers. Over 100,000 people registered in Yankton, Chamberlain, Fairfax, and Bonesteel for the 2600, 160-acre tracts of land. More than 30,000 registered in

Bonesteel alone. Bonesteel, a dangerous place for the ordinary citizen, now populated with 6,500 people, crawled with thugs of the underworld in search of easy money. Gamblers, gunmen, and robbers preyed on the unsuspecting. Thirteen saloons lined the crime-infested streets with its share of undesirable elements. Tired of living in fear and having their town taken over by crooks, the citizens of the town organized and would drive the unwanted infiltrators out in the Battle of Bonesteel.

In the searing heat of August, Frank, Marie, Vaclav, and Barbara travel to Spencer to welcome more family members to America. The Freemont, Elkhorn, and Missouri Valley Railroad has now reached Spencer making travel more convenient. Red, like the shining scarlet hips of the wild rose, a newly built depot stretches across a hilltop overlooking the wooded ravines of the Ponca Valley below. Oaks, box elders, cottonwoods, elms, willows, wild plums, chokecherry bushes, and grape vines wash the hillsides in fading hues.

*Josef* (Joseph) who traveled back to Bohemia earlier, returns with his wife *Mari* (Mary), his twenty-year-old brother *Matyas* (Mike), and his eighteen-year-old sister *Ruzena* (Roo-shee-nah) (Rosie). They hail each other using their old familiar Bohemian names, but they have assumed American names now since their arrival to America. Using these names will take some getting use to. Frank is still *Frantisek* (FRAHN-tee-shek) to them. Vaclav will retain his given name, although some of his friends and relatives will give him the nickname Jim or shorten his given name to Vac. (Marie will change hers to Mary but reassumes her given name with the American pronunciation after a period of time.)

*Spencer Depot.*

Marie rushes forward to embrace her mother, Barbara, a slight woman of a mere 80 pounds, whom she has not seen for two years.

"Let me hold my new grandson," says Barbara as she picks up the year old boy and gives him a squeeze."

Vaclav's wife, Barbara, hugs her sixteen-year-old sister, *Maria* and their mother also named *Maria*. They, too, have come across the ocean from the port of Bremen with Mike, Joseph, Mary, Barbara, and Rosie on the 'Kaiser Wilhelm II' to Ellis Island.

The newly arrived family settles into the area that is much drier and warmer than their homeland. But they adjust and forget these small discomforts, overshadowed by visions of a better life and the joy of being reunited with loved ones.

❦ ❦ ❦

One year later in August 1905, Frank, Vaclav and Mike file on adjoining 160-acre homesteads in the newly opened

Rosebud Reservation paying $2.50 per acre along with a four-teen dollar filing fee. Final proof can be made in five years or a patent can be obtained after eight months of actual residence when the full purchase price is paid and proof of residence given. The three brothers leave for their claim during the fall to set up homesteads to fulfill the requirements of establishing a residence within six months of the filing.

The women and children stay on the homestead in Spencer waiting for the men to return. While the men are gone, the women take on a task that Marie had started when she first came to Nebraska.

Marie left for America without the traditional dowry of a featherbed and a pair of feather pillows, because they were much too bulky to take on a journey across the ocean. After arriving in Nebraska, she has been raising geese to ensure feathers for plucking in early and late summer, as well as a traditional goose for Christmas dinner. Her neighbors and friends have saved their extra feathers for her, which she has stored away. After the three years in Spencer, she has almost enough feathers for a featherbed.

Marie locks the geese in the pen overnight so they will be ready for plucking in the morning. "I'm ready to go," announces Marie's mother at the first sign of breaking day as she adds an extra sleeve on her already covered arm for added protection from the quick nip of a goose.

"As soon as Barbara arrives, we will begin. I hope she brings over the young girls to catch the geese so we won't have to stop with the picking. In the meantime, let's take some wooden boxes out to the pen so we have something to sit on," says Marie.

The bewildered geese flap their wings and honk their piercing cry, resentful from being locked away from their favorite meadow.

"Geese make such a mess," observes Marie while dumping the odorous, dirty swill out of their pan and refilling it with fresh water."

"We're here," calls Barbara carrying something wrapped in a white cloth. "I brought some apple strudel to go with coffee later." She enters the pen with the two young girls, Rosie and Mary, all ready to catch the geese.

The experienced feather pickers take a seat and cover their laps with an old shirt or dress. With a flurry of feathers, honking and dust, they each take hold of a caught goose by the feet, right side up, and carefully tuck its long neck under an arm. At first the goose resists, but determining there's no harm intended, it remains still while the women pull the downy feathers from the breast, back, base of the neck and from around the wings. The partially denuded fowl elicits a few chuckles from the girls upon its release.

"The feathers will grow back in time for cold weather," reassures Marie's mother.

Finally, the ordeal concludes. "Time for coffee. Let's wash up and go in," suggests Marie.

Apple strudel, coffee, bags of feathers, and a good visit make the day worthwhile. Now Marie has enough feathers to stuff the ticking for her featherbed.

After several weeks, the brothers return. Marie, anxious to learn about the new home site, plies Frank with questions on his return.

"The land looks much like it does around here with the rolling river hills, though not as many trees," he tells her. "It

*South Dakota, 1908.*

isn't settled yet so it looks a little lonely. When we got there to start putting up the buildings, a cold wind was blowing fiercely across the land. Even the coyotes took to their dens and snakes had slithered into their holes. So we did what the prairie creatures do and made a dugout for shelter in the side of a hill in a low draw facing northeast near the Missouri River. We managed to put up two small, rather crude, sod houses for Mike and us. We cut some hay as well. Now all we have to do is bide our time until spring, then Vac and his family will leave with us. Mike says he will come later."

Frank's parents, their daughter Barbara and her son, the last of the family to leave Bohemia, arrive in Spencer by train during the fall of 1905. Frank's father comes to this new country at the age of 55 with one hundred dollars to begin all over again. They live with son Joseph and Mary since they have no children and have room for the newcomers. Frank and Marie enjoy their company for about five months before they part ways again.

*Chapter Three*

# Leaving for the Rosebud

Several months later, in March of 1906, after five years of renting, Frank, Marie, Vaclav, and Barbara as well as their children finally leave Nebraska for South Dakota. Marie's mother and Charley stay behind with the rest of the relatives. Frank will come for his mother-in-law and son later. The wagon jolts along hitting another gopher hole jarring Marie out of her pensive mood. She looks back and picks up baby Anna off the feather tick in the back of the wagon.

The wagons follow yet another meandering Indian trail made by the nomadic Lakota Indians, also known as the Sioux, a name given to them by the French, meaning enemy. Preferring to be called the Lakota or Dakota, they inhabited the region now open for settlement. The Great Sioux Reservation to which the Lakota were placed in 1877 occupied most of western South Dakota. Twelve years later another agreement reduced the reservation further into six smaller reservations, the Rosebud being one of them. The government offered the surplus land for sale.

No established roads exist out here yet, only trails criss-crossing each other and disappearing over the hills. Frank points out a trail in the distance. "See that trail, Marie, it leads to Ft. Pierre and Chamberlain."

Marie can't help wondering about the forlorn absence of trees. The treeless prairie offers little solace to those accustomed to the peaceful stability of trees, but Frank assures her this treeless prairie is composed of fertile soil. "Just look at this grass. Have you ever seen anything like it?" asks Frank. "Buffalo thrived on these gramma, buffalo, and wheat grasses. Surely our few cows will do the same."

"Yes, that may be, but it is also a good hiding place for snakes," says Marie. She wonders about the adaptability of the Indians who had lived here for years subsisting largely on buffalo, deer, and other small game supplemented by berries and other plants they could gather. "What will happen to the Indians?"

"The government promises they will pay the Indians for whatever land is purchased by the homesteaders, like us, and placed into a trust fund for the Lakota people," says Frank.

Here and there cottonwood stakes stand tall and foreign sticking out of the ground marking the sections. Large rocks mark the quarters serving as a guide to help the homesteaders in finding their coveted piece of land. Marie and Frank don't pay close attention to them today, as Frank knows exactly where to go.

In the distance, purple-blue buttes sweep up out of the prairie breaking the monotony of the landscape to the north. "See those buttes Marie? We are getting close."

The gentle rolling hills continue to dip and swell before them. After a time, Frank reins his four-horse team to the east. Over the first rise, Marie gazes on serene river hills breaking to the southeast. A glimpse of the Missouri shimmers behind a high ridge. Frank stops the wagon at the top of the hill and points to the east. "Over there is our claim."

Marie holds her hand above her brow and strains her eyes to see the place that will be her home for the next fifty-four years. "Yes, yes I think I can see the soddy." But the strong wind at the top of the hill reminds her that this land holds a defying strength.

Before them extend limitless open spaces virtually untouched by human hands, although many adventure seekers have passed this way before leaving a trail of history. The Missouri served as a waterway of adventure and exploration for Lewis and Clark, fur traders, Indians, military men, princes, artists, desperadoes, and other adventure seekers. All had a rendezvous with the river. Now, two undaunted pioneers are ready to add to the pages of history. The limitless vistas might be daunting to some, but to them it means freedom to search for a dream or perhaps a challenge in defining the human spirit. Only the strong and resilient are a match for the untamed land.

In a short time, the brothers and their families arrive at their claims. The families wave to one another and divide routes. Vaclav and Barbara proceed a little further to their dugout to the northeast. Frank and Marie plod along to the east where after a time they pull up to the soddy. The sod house looks inviting after several days in a wagon. With Anna in her arms, Marie hurriedly jumps down from the wagon anxious to unpack the wagon and set up housekeeping. "Frank, check the soddy for unwelcome visitors. Snakes or mice could have moved in over the winter to den up in the walls," Marie suggests as she props the hoe near the doorway. The hoe will be ready and waiting to deliver a fatal blow to the menacing rattlesnake, quite plentiful on the prairie. Killing several dozen in a summer was not unheard of in the early days. Some of the unlucky homesteaders that were bitten did not always recover from snakebite, and those that did went through an agonizing healing process.

"No snakes in here," Frank shouts back. "There may be a few mice hiding, but I can't find them just now. They're not about to show themselves."

Satisfied that no surprises await them, the couple begins to unload the wagon and set up the stove and the beds. Marie surveys the soddy after everything is moved in. "This is really going to be crowded," she says.

"It will only be temporary. We will build a larger soddy later," Frank promises.

Marie decides it will be a waste of time to plaster the walls with a mixture of clay and ashes or to whitewash them. And she doesn't have any newspapers to paper the walls. Maybe she will before the next sod house is built. She also makes a mental note that she will try and get some cheesecloth, unbleached muslin, or oil cloth on their visit to the prairie town to hang on the ceiling and the windows to keep out dirt and bugs from dropping in on them unexpectedly.

In spite of the cramped quarters, the thick sod walls will keep them warm in the cool months and cool in the warm months. With curtains on the windows, a potted plant or two on the wide windowsills, and canvas or rugs on the dirt floor, a soddy seems like it will be quite cozy until a downpour of rain anyway. Since their roof consists of branches, twigs, and sod, a leaking roof is almost a certainty.

Tired from their journey, they fall into bed oblivious to the howling serenade of the coyotes. The next morning they awaken to Anna's whimpers. A bright new day challenges their newfound energy. Before Frank can begin work on the homestead, he has to make preparations to return to Spencer to bring Marie's mother Barbara and young son Charley, two years of age, as well as more of their belongings back to their new home. Vaclav will accompany Frank on the return trip.

The women and children will stay behind, together, in the dugout. For now, the horses have to rest a few more days before they can leave. In the meantime, the men cut wood from the creek bottoms so the women will have fuel for their fires. They also hunt for wild game they can leave with their families. The game can be salted down to preserve it for future use.

Marie, in her apprehension about the men leaving them out on the prairie alone, tries to keep herself occupied. She bakes bread, *chleba*, so the men will have food to take along. Fear tugs at her as she kneads the bread. The men will be gone at least a week or more if they run into difficulties. March blizzards can come up fast without much warning. The wagons will need to be loaded and the horses must rest before they begin their journey back. Questions keep nagging at the back of her mind. What if something goes wrong out on the claim? What if the children become sick? They are miles away from the nearest neighbor and about nine miles away from the nearest frontier town. Well it has to be. This was decided long ago.

Marie frets about whether Frank is dressed warmly enough or has enough food with him for the journey. She always feels better when she is with him making sure everything is done the way it should be. "Please be careful and hurry back as soon as you can," she pleads.

"Now remember, don't leave the dugout if a storm come up," warns Frank.

Marie watches as the men leave the homestead. The wagons gently creak across the prairie disappearing over the first hill. She busies herself with the cooking, cleaning, and washing and taking care of Anna to help pass the time. Each day she ventures out to milk and feed the cows they brought with them.

Towards the end of the week, the skies in the west grow dark gray and the air temperature grows colder. The air tingles with a sense of foreboding. The women agree a storm is imminent and prepare for it. Marie scurries around bringing in fuel for the stove, the icy snowflakes stinging her face. She must feed the livestock before she goes into the house. She enters the crude shelter built for them and pushes them hay that Frank and Vaclav had cut in the fall. Before going into the house, she secures a rope to the shelter and strings it along to the house. No telling how difficult this storm will get. She and Barbara may not be able to tend the livestock without a rope to guide them in a blinding blizzard. Frank's departing words ring in her ear. She will see how the storm progresses. By the time she returns to the house, the howling wind has picked up. The snow starts swirling in every direction. The women and children remain safe in the dugout as long as they don't venture far outside. But what about the returning family? Are they, too, caught in a blizzard? Fences do not exist out here yet to guide the travelers and prevent them from becoming lost. Fear grips Marie's heart. Never

*Site of dugout (note depression to the right). Photo courtesy of Bob Brozik*

again does she want to be left alone. The blizzard rages and shrieks for two days and two nights.

Marie grows impatient on waiting for the men to return and finds herself pacing the floor. She looks out the small front window only to see that it is covered with snow.

"Barbara, I think we are buried under drifts," says Marie frightened as she tries the door.

They open the door just a little. "There's a wall of snow out there. How are we going to get out?" says Barbara trying not to panic.

"When the storm dies down, we will have to dig our way out. I just hope the stovepipe doesn't fill up with snow before then or we will smother in this hole." The women sit quietly watching the stove for signs of smoke.

They can only guess how much time has passed. The dark interior makes it difficult to distinguish between night and day. The dirt walls crowd in closer and closer. Marie glances towards the lamp flickering on the table. She notices that there isn't much kerosene left. "Do you think it's getting harder to breathe in here?" Marie asks Barbara.

"No, I think we are all right. Our nerves are just getting the best of us. I hear something. Listen," says Barbara quietly.

"Someone's digging. I think."

"Marie, Barbara, are you all right in there?" Frank's voice penetrates the wall of snow.

"Yes, yes, we are fine. Hurry and get us out of here," Marie yells to him.

Finally, after a restless wait, the men reach the doorway. In a flutter of excitement, the family members greet one another, relieved that everyone is well and has survived the days apart.

Marie, overcome with emotion, can barely speak. She lifts her two-year-old son, Charley, up and looks him over. "My I think you have grown." This is all she can manage to say.

"We couldn't find the dugout," says Frank breathlessly. "Everything is covered in snow. One hills looks like another. Luckily, Vac spotted the chimney sticking out the snow bank. We were so afraid you might all have suffocated." After calming himself down from the excitement, he catches his breath and continues. "We traveled the hill tops to avoid the deep snow in the bottoms. Our other wagon is about two miles back. The horses were so played out pulling the heavy load that we had to unhitch the wagon and leave it. We will go after it in the morning."

"Come on and warm yourselves while I make you all something to eat," Barbara offers.

"I'll unhitch the horses first and take care of them, and then I will be in," says Frank.

"I'm so glad we spent many Nebraska winter evenings putting feather ticks together. We would have been stiff with cold without them on the trip," says Marie's mother as she looks around the snug dugout. "I didn't know for awhile if we would make it. This is even more desolate than Nebraska."

After a warm meal, Frank and his family leave for the soddy. Several more storms hit before spring arrives. Each snowstorm worries the new settlers. Frank and Marie make it a practice to look across the prairie and check to see that Vaclav's dugout is not snowed under again. Vaclav vows that in the spring he will build a soddy too.

*Chapter Four*

# Settling In

Several months pass before the last of the snow melts in the warming sun. Rivulets of water trickle into creek beds. The fresh smell of the warming earth mingles with the sweet smell of plum bushes blooming in the canyons. The desire to stop and reflect on the miracle of spring has to be put aside for now. Much work needs to be done before next winter.

Frank sharpens the plowshare, dulled after plowing through the tough roots, by inverting it and pounding the edge thinner with a hammer. He uses a file to make it even sharper. This will do until he can take it to a blacksmith who heats the share first, making for a finer edge. The Homestead Act requires five acres to be broken the first year with a breaking plow and a team of horses, but Frank intends to break more. With his team of three to four horses and a fourteen inch plow, he can break up to one or two acres a day.

Marie walks out to the field with morning coffee and watches the plow, agriculture's most important tool, change the landscape forever. Ribbons of glistening black earth roll upward out of the ground. The tenacious roots resist the plow with all their might, refusing to be ripped from the earth like a child clinging to his mother. Breaking sod between May and June rots the roots properly, increasing the chance of good crop production the following spring. At the end of the plowed ground, Frank stops to let the horses rest. Marie pours the hot coffee into tin cups as they breathe in deeply of the freshly turned earth.

"Tomorrow we should be able to plant corn," Frank predicts. He chooses corn as the first crop, like most settlers, because it is easy to plant and harvest, and weeds aren't a problem on the newly turned sod.

"With mother here to watch the children, I should be able to help you," offers Marie as she places the lid back on the coffee jar. "We also need to plant cabbage and potatoes. It's getting a little late for potatoes, but they still should do well in the newly turned sod."

"Don't forget the bean and pea seed we brought from Nebraska," reminds Frank as he picks up the rich fragrant soil in his hands. "They should do well also."

"We will need all the vegetables we can raise to see us through the winter. If only the rains will come when we need them."

Frank nods in agreement. After consuming his coffee, he returns to his plowing. Marie picks up the empty coffee jar and returns to the house. She lifts her face to the warm sun grateful that winter has released its chilling grip. The gentle breeze blows through her hair and playfully ruffles her skirt. The intoxicating promise of spring reaffirms that they have made the right decision to come to South Dakota. With planting in mind, she decides to prepare her seed potatoes for the ground. Luckily they fared the trip without freezing. After finding a sharp knife, she carries her bag of potatoes outside. Sitting down she takes her knife and cuts the sprouted potatoes into sections, each with a healthy sprout. She also sews a special apron that will hold plenty of seed so she can help Frank plant the corn. She, too, loves to take part in the planting process, nurturing seeds to full plant growth.

As Frank promises, the next day they begin their planting, first the potatoes and then the corn. They carefully place the sprouted sections of potatoes in the warming ground sprout side up and cover them with the fertile soil. Frank uses a hand planter, also known as a stabber, to plant the corn. Made of boards with steel points on the end, it reaches as high as his belt. Marie places some of the kernels out of her apron into a metal container towards the top of the planter. Frank then jabs the point of the hand planter into the turned earth while pushing the upper end of the device together releasing a certain number of seeds into the ground. Marie steps on the slit made by the hand planter to close up the ground so it retains the moisture necessary for the seed to germinate.

In June, Frank turns his attention to the haying. He tightly holds the long wooden handle of the scythe. Using his brawny strength, he swings the scythe cutting the fragrant hay with the sharp curved blade. "You need a mowing machine to make the work easier," says Marie as she approaches him in the hay field.

"You can be sure I will buy or borrow one next year," says Frank as he prepares to swing his scythe one more time. "The tall, thick grass will make good winter feed for the livestock after it is cured and stacked. We can even burn the twisted hay if we run short on fuel this winter."

"That will probably be unlikely with all the wood near the river," says Marie.

With the haying completed, once again Frank plows for the purpose of sod building. Building with wood is much too expensive for a settler with little money, and besides they are miles from the nearest railroad to bring in the lumber. Under Marie's watchful eye, he stacks the sod to form a chicken house.

"Build it a little bigger," commands Marie as she helps him to determine the length. "Chickens don't like to be crowded."

"When this is finished you won't have to worry about coyotes and badgers getting your hens, *slepice*. They will also be safe from the elements. As soon as I'm finished, here, I'll start on a shelter for the horses and cows."

"Will it be of sod too?" says Marie.

"No, we will build it of poles, slew grass and woven wire. There's plenty of grass so we might as well make use of it."

They spend the first summer building up their homestead and tending their crops. Frank spends whatever time that is left constructing a larger sod house for the growing family. Marie helps in whatever way she can when she has the time. Frank chooses a spot with the thickest sod. First, he hays it and then plows it into furrows with his breaking plow and team of horses. They then use a spade to cut the sod into three-foot brick lengths, which they stack in brick laying fashion after they have determined the size of the house. Marie fills the cracks between the sod with a clay mixture. Frank brings up wood from the river to frame the windows and doorway. Since this house will be used for some time, they have decided on a wooden roof, which will be covered with sod for added protection from the rain and snow. Soon grasses, cactus, and sunflowers will grow on the sod-covered roof blending it well into the prairie scene. "I will get Vac to help me set the heavy posts on either side of the house to support the ridge poles that will hold up the roof," says Frank.

The young couple agrees to add a wood floor to the house. Even the most fastidious of sod dweller housewives complain of the intruding, nibbling fleas, and bedbugs that like to hide in the dirt, grass roofs, and the crevices of the sod blocks. Using as much wood in the construction of the sod house as possible, and whitewashing or plastering the walls, help to eliminate the problem. Also, Marie can scrub the wood floors clean.

Marie feels comforted to have her mother nearby to help care for the children while she is helping Frank build up the homestead and take care of the daily chores which are always in abundance. Cooking and cleaning alone take up much of her time. But there are so many other things she must do for them to survive out here so far from anywhere.

Daily, she saves the ashes from the stove. When she acquires enough, she pours water over them and lets them set. After a time she pours the water off. She mixes the lye that is left with lard or tallow, pours it in a large pan, and lets it set. The mixture hardens into soap that she cuts into squares. She uses this homemade soap for all her cleaning needs.

At the break of day, Marie hauls in water that she has taken out of the water barrels to heat on the stove in a large boiler for the weekly wash. She uses the precious water spar-

ingly, careful not to waste a single drop. Frank has constructed wood strips to divert rainwater from the roof to barrels
beside the house. Although the water comes out of the eaves
mixed with dirt from the sod, it will eventually settle. The
soft water combined with her lye soap makes for a quick lath-
er. She always reserves some rainwater for washing her hair,
since it always leaves it so soft. Unfortunately, the water does
not last long, causing Frank to make a trip to the river to
bring back barrels of water.

Marie pours the heated water into a washtub outside and
places her washboard upright in the water. She takes the
soiled clothes and scrubs them vigorously on the washboard
until she is satisfied they are clean. She then places the
clothes in another tub of clean water to be rinsed. Arms stiff
from scrubbing, she looks up to see Frank coming across the
prairie with a rabbit and prairie chickens fastened to his belt,
his gun propped up against his shoulder. With a pleased voice
and a boyish grin on his face he calls to Marie, "Here's meat
for dinner." Frank delights in this newfound freedom of hunt-
ing whenever he likes.

"If you clean them, I'll fry them up with prairie onions. It's
been awhile since we have had meat. With gravy and
dumplings they will be a treat."

"I've been too busy lately to hunt, but I spotted some
prairie chickens this morning and couldn't resist."

Her busy day continues into the twilight hours. Marie
must bring in the cows that roam free during the day with no
fences to stop them. The soft breath of the earth whispers
cool against her face as she descends into a draw. The over
waist-high coarse grass cuts against her clothing while swal-
lowing up her small form as she walks to bring in the cows.

She searches for a well-worn cow path so she is better able to see what lies ahead of her. She clutches the club she always takes with her and cringes as she places one foot in front of the other. Was that the deadly buzz of a rattler? No just a grasshopper. "If only I had a dog to walk ahead of me," she wishes to herself.

As the summer wears on, the heat and wind become unbearable at times. Even though Marie enjoys being out-doors, she seeks the cool respite of the soddy during the hottest part of the day. During the evening hours the wind and heat abate, then Marie and her mother bring the cranky, confined children outside. They spread a quilt on the ground and watch the children so they don't venture off in the tall grass. Marie takes this opportunity to rest awhile since she is expecting another child. She doesn't remember ever being so tired as she is right now. The work seems endless and no com-forts abound, but her energy and determination exceed the slightness of her physical being.

Marie looks out across the fireguard that Frank plowed earlier this spring. Not only does the family keep their eyes on the clouds watching for sign of rain, *prset*, or storm clouds threatening to send pounding hail on their crops, but they also scan the horizon for smoke. Environmental elements rule their lives. Possible calamity lurks with the dawning of each new day. Rain, imperative to prosperity and even sur-vival, often does not come in the form of a gentle rain. More often it is accompanied by fierce winds and lightning that cracks like whips, ablaze with fire, often touching off prairie fires in the tall, tinder dry grass. Aided by the wind, it will destroy everything in its path quickly. Frank keeps pails for water and gunnysacks handy to beat out any encroaching flames.

The first year on the homestead, the young couple reaps a harvest of vegetables and corn. The wind sends rain and promise for prosperity. Being young and healthy to cope with the daily demands of the prairie makes life a little easier.

Marie harvests the surplus from her garden. She has no canning jars to preserve the extra produce. Instead, she dries the beans and the peas and shreds the cabbage for sauerkraut. During dinner one day she reminds Frank, "You will need to dig a root cellar before winter to store the potatoes and some of the cabbage as well as the cream and milk. Besides, I like a place to go when the ferocious spring storms hit. The pamphlets we read in Bohemia never said anything about the violent prairie storms or the intense heat."

"I'll see if I can get Vac and Mike to come over and help me. Mike should be caught up with his work. He did get a late start by arriving a few weeks after we did. But we can help him out too, if he's behind."

The trio of brothers, driven by the impending onset of winter, work diligently digging the root cellar. Since Frank's parents have decided to leave Nebraska and will come to live near their sons, he decides to dig a well also. Hauling water from the river creates a burden especially in the winter when the river freezes over.

The brothers practice the art of water witching to locate a vein of water. Frank searches for a Y-shaped willow branch, the only equipment needed for water witching. Although none of them has acquired much experience in the technique, Marie hopes that one of the men has the special gift to feel the pull towards water while holding the willow.

Taking the two branches of the forked willow in his hand, Frank walks slowly with the willow held out horizontally before him. He divines close to the house and around the buildings; carefully concentrating, he lets the rod guide him. When he's about to question his ability for divining, to everyone's surprise, the free end of the fork drops down indicating a location of water.

"You try it Mike and see what happens," says Frank, a little skeptical of his find.

Mike's search delivers the same results, and they all agree this is the place to begin digging.

"I hope we don't hit a vein of alkaline water," says Vaclav. "It isn't fit for any living thing."

Frank takes a spade and begins to dig a hole about thirty inches in diameter. Mike and Vaclav join in with shovels and picks digging down as far as they can. They curb the first three feet of the well with boards to prevent a cave in from the top of the well. They can dig no further until they devise a windlass. The men set two posts, notched like forks, on either side of the well. They place a straight log across the forked posts, attaching a rope and a bucket to the log. Since Frank's small build will fit nicely into the pit, and because this is his well, the brothers lower him slowly into the shaft using the windlass so he can resume digging.

"Be careful so nothing comes down on my head," shouts Frank from the depth of the well.

Marie scurries across the yard carrying a lantern. She stops at the well and inspects the rope. "There are no frayed spots on the rope are there, Vac?"

"No, we checked it over carefully. It's sound as can be."

•

"I brought a lantern that you can light and lower into the well later when Frank gets deeper. There could be damp in the well. If the light is snuffed out, then you know there's bad air."

The men nod to her in acknowledgement. "I don't think we will be going that deep," says Vaclav.

Frank jerks on the rope as a signal to haul up another bucket of dirt. A rock accidentally dislodges on the rim of the hole.

"Watch out Frank," yells Mike.

"Frank, are you all right?" screams Marie, panic stricken as she peers over the edge.

A weak "Yes," reaches to the top. "I flattened myself against the wall. The rock just missed me. I told you all to be careful."

"I can't watch anymore of this," says Marie as she leaves for the house.

After several days of toiling in the deep pit, Frank reaches the sandy layer and useable water starts to flow. The brothers turn the windlass and haul Frank out of the hole. Now they must make a cover for the well.

❦ ❦ ❦

Summer begins to fade. The breeze blows through the somber yellow-brown grasses. "How would you like to go and see a powwow?" says Frank one late summer day during the afternoon coffee.

"Are we welcome?" says Marie.

"Lots of settlers in the area have been invited and have gone. They say it's interesting."

"Well all right. We'll take mother and the children too. They might enjoy it."

"They begin with the dancing just before sundown, so be ready."

The darkening night awakens to the primordial beat of Indian drums, pulsating ancient tribal songs across the prairie hills. Frank and the family approach the flat-topped buttes. A circular structure, erected by the Lakota Indians, symbolic of the sacred hoop of the nation, poses below near Bull Creek. Newly cut brush forms a canopy on the outer rim of the circle to provide shade and seating. The sacred dancing has already commenced in the center of the ring. The native people enjoy themselves celebrating, dancing, singing, visiting, and renewing the old ways as well as preserving traditions of their heritage. Settlers, unaccustomed to this culture, shyly approach the ring. They come to satisfy their curiosity.

Frank and the family find a place to sit under the arbor. The children, not quite sure what to think, stay close by their parents' side.

Firelight reflects on faces intent on the dance. The traditional male dancers dressed in their leggings, buckskins, and feathered bonnets dance slowly with their heads bobbing up and down while glancing from side to side. Traditional women in buckskin dresses, decorated with bone, shell, and beads, dip and sway to the beat of the drum.

The lead singers change the pace of the drumbeat throughout the night. Songs and dances portray animals and nature. Some male dancers imitate the hopping of a crow. The dancer's foot hits the ground with each strike of the rawhide drum. The drumbeat changes again as dancers gracefully move and bend while holding strands of braided sweet grass. The dancers sway with the music like long blades of prairie grass blowing in the wind. Although Frank and Marie do not understand the significance of the dances, they find them fascinating.

The evening of dancing and celebrating concludes with the round dance. Frank motions to Marie that he will be right back as he quietly slips away. A little bewildered, she watches some of the visitors accept the invitation to participate in the round dance. They all join hands and move in a clockwise direction like the sun. The dance signifies the bond of friendship strengthening the circle.

After the round dance, Frank reappears with a puppy. "For you," he says handing the soft, cuddly creature to Marie. "A companion to protect you from the rattlers. Dogs can tear a snake apart, you know."

"How did you get it?" she says.

"I asked an Indian using a kind of sign language to see if I could buy a dog. With my Bohemian and his Lakota, we weren't getting anywhere. They have plenty of dogs around. He just gave me one."

Anna and Charley appeal with their eager arms to hold the puppy. Granted their wish, they nuzzle their faces into its soft fur.

The cycle of the seasons flows uninterrupted. Winter descends across the bleak and barren plains. Snug in the newly built sod house, Marie awaits the birth of her third child. The long winter evenings provide the opportunity for more leisurely pursuits. After supper, Marie and her mother spend their time mending and patching work worn clothing or remaking over a garment for one of the children by the flickering light of the kerosene lamp. Out of muslin cloth flour and seed sacks, Marie fashions a few new baby things. When Marie's mother finishes the mending and the patching, she cuts up squares out of clothing no longer serviceable, which she sews into a quilt. Frank repairs harnesses and whittles toys out of wood for the children.

"Charley, come over here. I have something for you," coaxes Frank as he finishes up his latest project.

A wide grin appears on the young lad's face as he grips the toy wooden gun.

"Me, too?" pleads Anna.

"All right, I'll make you one too." Frank laughs at their obvious pleasure. "I have done enough whittling tonight. Now if I can loosen up my fingers I'll play some music," he says as he takes the accordion out of its case. "What shall I play?"

"Play a polka," requests Marie. "The children love to dance."

The lively, toe tapping music and laughter of little children lifts the blanket of silence covering the prairie night.

On a cold day in February, Marie sends Frank to fetch her sister-in-law, Barbara, from the nearby claim.

"Are you sure you don't want me to go after a doctor?" offers Frank

"Barbara and I have helped with each other's births, and we have done all right as midwives. I would rather have her than a strange doctor. Besides, it would take too long to get him, and he's probably away taking care of all the young families in the area. Take the children along with you to Vac's. Mother will stay here with me. You all can stay with him until this is all over. Now hurry, this might go faster than the others."

Several hours later the family returns to find a wrinkled-wee baby in the arms of his mother.

"What shall we name him?" asks Frank looking down on his second son.

"Let's give him your name. I don't know how many more boys we will have," says Marie. "Take him and put him in the cradle. I'm exhausted."

Marie's mother strokes her daughter's forehead before she lifts the baby from his mother's arms. As she lays him in the cradle she says, "The name *Frantisek* means free. You are lucky little one to be born into such a country."

After much discussion over the winter months, Marie's mother applies for citizenship, renouncing allegiance to Francis Joseph, Emperor of Austria, a requirement to own land. Then on April 22, 1907, at the age of 57, she files on a homestead one mile to the east of Frank's claim.

Prior to the Homestead Act of 1862, very few women were permitted to own land. During the 1840's single and widowed women have brought suits against the government to uphold their rights to the public domain allowing some women to break the patriarchal control. Some courts have recognized their rights. But it was the Homestead Act, a major piece of legislation, which has allowed more women to own property.

Barbara, like many single or widowed women, decides to file on a claim as a way of obtaining more land or as an investment, provided she can prove up the claim in five years. The law requires that married couples stay on their land, but an exception is made for the single occupant recognizing that they may need to work elsewhere to support the endeavor. Barbara has to live on her claim a few days a week to satisfy the requirements.

When weather permits, the men build a two-room shanty from rough lumber brought across the river by ferry. They build it on a grassy point extending to the south overlooking the ravines and violet green hills of the Missouri River breaks. Here she lives several nights a week satisfying the residency requirements. In the meantime, Frank breaks the land.

"Are you sure you want to stay here alone?" asks Marie as she helps her mother get settled.

"Yes, I am getting used to the prairie," assures Marie's mother.

"But you have always been surrounded by people. In the Old Country, villages were close together. You never wanted for company. Even in Nebraska, we were together."

"It will only be a few days a week. Don't worry," Barbara tells her.

Marie puts the dishes away in the makeshift cupboard and lays out the patchwork quilt on the bed. "We must leave soon. It's getting late and Frank will be coming for us." Marie bundles up young Frank for the ride home. "Children, tell your grandmother, *Babicka*, goodbye."

*Babicka* will be over soon to read you Bible stories," she says as she gives each child a hug.

Marie looks back with concern on her face wondering how her mother could stay out here all alone. "Watch for snakes! You know they can be anywhere."

"Don't fret. I will be careful, and I have my Bible for comfort," her mother reassures her as she waves her away.

Twilight begins to paint the western sky with streaks of crimson. A coyote howls from shadowed hills as a mournful wind blows across the flatland from the north. *Babicka* stands at the door and watches as they climb into the wagon and disappear from sight.

≋ ≋ ≋

Several months later, Frank hitches the horses to the buggy in preparation for a trip to Dixon, the closest prairie town, for supplies and a little diversion from the monotony of work and landscape. Since they won't be buying large amounts of supplies, the buggy will do and will be much faster than the clumsy and slow wagon. *Babicka* agrees to watch the children for the day.

Marie fills the cream can with the cream she has kept cool in the cave. She tucks a few more eggs in the egg crate carefully supervising Frank as he loads the buggy.

They wave goodbye to the children as they prepare to leave. Frank lets the exhilarated horses run. Their manes fly in the wind. "Slow down," Marie says with frustration. "The cream will be surely churned to butter, and the eggs will be scrambled before we get there. I would like to get there in one piece myself."

Frank pulls back on the reins giving Marie a wink.

They travel southwest across the prairie on a bright summer morn. More homesteads come into view as the morning wears on, certainly many more than when they first came to this country.

The trip passes quickly as Frank and Marie discuss changes they view along the way. Dixon, a thriving community with over 100 occupants, established in 1904 as a trading point for the newly settled region, now comes into view. The crudely fashioned, but optimistic buildings spring up out of the prairie, lightening the hearts of the weary travelers.

They notice a newly built church and a school upon entering the town. About two hundred Indian tepees ring the outskirts of Dixon. Under hastily constructed arbors of poles and brush, the Indians wait for their allotment checks. In a short time, Marie and Frank stop in front of the general store where Frank unloads the cream and eggs to be traded for merchandise. Before they begin their day in town, Frank takes the buggy and team to the livery stable where the horses will be fed and watered during their stay. Frank doesn't often indulge in this extravagance, but it has been a long trip for the horses.

Marie alights from the buggy and begins her adventure in town leaving Frank to his errands. She hears a ringing dinner bell from the nearby hotel. Perhaps some affluent homesteaders who are waiting for their house to be built on their claim are pulling up chairs to the table, maybe a drummer selling his wares is in town, or someone waiting for the next stage is enjoying a prepared meal in the hotel. Marie catches a glimpse of the interior elegance of the hotel with its bright colored wallpaper, oak furniture, fine tablecloths, and matching dinnerware. The meager lunch she has packed seems a little drab in comparison.

She continues on down the street, the boardwalk ringing under her feet as she passes the bank, general store, and butcher shop on her way to the post office. Fine sleek horses tied to the hitching rails impatiently stamp their feet freeing themselves of pesky flies. Anxious to see if any mail has

arrived on the stage from Bonesteel and Gregory, she chooses this as her first stop before she does her shopping.

Just before she reaches the post office she hears laughter
and loud voices along with a dank odor of stale beer drifting
from the saloon. She has heard stories that this establishment
can get quite rowdy, and it has the bullet holes in the deco-
rative tin walls to prove them. She hastens her step and
arrives at the post office finding that she has a letter from a
friend living in Chicago. She places it in her pocket for safe
keeping so she can read it later, savoring every word.

First, she must shop. Two general stores, one on either side
of the street, provide the necessities for the homesteader. She
first chooses Steel and Campbell where Frank unloaded the
cream and eggs.

The gentle squeak of the screen door welcomes her as she
steps across the threshold. When she enters the store, wonderful smells of pickle barrels, freshly ground coffee beans,
leather, and new wood rise up to meet her. She glances to the
left at the shoe department with its highly polished, iron-
framed fold down chairs. Sturdy work boots and glossy, high-
buttoned shoes line the shelves. She looks down at her dull,
dusty worn shoes. They will have to do for a while longer.

Bolts of cloth, calicos and gingham, are piled high on
shelves behind a counter conveniently placed for measuring
and cutting. The clerk mounts brown paper on a metal roller
to one end of counter ready for use. A large cabinet hides various sewing notions tucked away inside its multiple sized
drawers. Marie selects a yard of bright cheery flower sprigged
calico for an apron and some thread. The clerk neatly wraps
her purchase in brown paper and deftly ties it with string.

Throughout the store, cabinets display various items from books to dishes enticing the customers. She continues to feast her eyes·on the bright and shiny new household items, crockery, and even store bought dresses, a pleasant change from the austere surroundings of her daily life. "Enough dawdling," she thinks to herself as she moves over to the food items behind the counter. Clumps of bananas hang suspended from the beams; barrels of apples and vinegar line the aisle. Even though Marie speaks only Bohemian, she manages to communicate to the clerk what she wants and in turn the clerk writes the purchases down on paper, adding them up and subtracting the amount for the cream and eggs. He rings up the transaction on a large ornate cash register commanding one end of the counter. She must be prudent with her buying as money is scarce.

A little disgruntled, she discovers Frank has not joined her in the store. She leaves her bundles momentarily while she goes and looks for him. She knows he enjoys a good visit with fellow Bohemians and finds him at the livery stable. "Where have you been?" says Marie in a rather irritated tone.

Frank looks a little sheepish, "I guess I lost track of time," he apologizes.

Marie softens a little, secretly smiles to herself realizing that he deserves to have some fun too. The livery stable as well as the saloon, the social gathering places for men, offers entertainment in the comings and goings of settlers and businessmen. The men discuss the weather, hire rigs, or ask for information about the area. She prefers finding him at the livery rather than the saloon. She hustles him along to eat their lunch and finish their shopping.

Before they leave town, they visit the newspaper office to see about running the required final proof notices in order to obtain the patent for their land. After they make the final payment, the land will be theirs before the five-year proving up period, provided two witnesses testify that improvements have been made and other conditions met. Frank learns that the newspaper charges a fee of six to ten dollars for running the notices six times before the patent is given. This brisk business with the newly settled region keeps the newspapers in business.

With their errands completed, they load their packages in the buggy and leave town down the long dusty streets. The sun begins its downward descent, but there is still time to stop for a visit with Mrs. Supik, a relative and another Bohemian settler. She and her family live outside of town. Maybe she has made some fresh prune filled kolaches to go with the afternoon coffee.

*Chapter Five*

# Family

The following year, Frank makes a trip to Gregory to pick up his parents, Vaclav and Barbara, arriving from Nebraska on the train. They have come to live near their sons. Soon Albert arrives in South Dakota from Nebraska to live with his parents and help with the work. Joseph and Mary leave Nebraska, too, and settle about fourteen miles to the south of Frank and Marie. They live there several years, but not finding prairie life to their liking, they move to Louisiana.

The brothers bring in lumber from the ferry and build a small frame house for their parents three quarters of a mile from Frank's place. The house is situated in a draw and protected from the winds. With so many family members nearby, Sunday gatherings become an important routine in their lives. Music, food, visiting, and an argument or two recreate the community of family and friends that they left behind in Bohemia.

The Bohemians, also referred to as Czechs, adjust to America more easily when they settle near family and friends, finding strength in unity. Frank and his brothers

*The Brass Band. Albert and Mike are to the right. Photo courtesy of Jim Beranek*

adjust well to the community of fellow Bohemians. Shortly after their arrival, the brothers organize a band with several other neighbors calling themselves The Brass Band. They play for many local gatherings, most often in sod houses, after moving the furniture out into the yard or to another building. An evening's rain shower occasionally dampens the nightly entertainment with a downpour of leaking mud from an ill built roof, but not for long. After scooping out the mud, the fun continues.

To further the solidarity of their culture, they organize lodges throughout the country. Frank, Joseph, Albert, and Vaclav join the ZCBJ lodge, *Zapadni Ceska Bratrska Jednota,* translated Western Fraternal Life Association. The *Zelena Hora,* Green Mountain order, established in Dixon organizes early after the first settlers arrive. The order is determined to preserve the Bohemian culture and language, which was repressed under Hapsburg rule in Bohemia. The ZCBJ offers social opportunities as well as provides insurance and advice to the Bohemian-speaking members. Through participation in the meetings, the members learn the democratic process of their new land of which they have become citizens. They begin to appreciate free speech and voting, rights repressed in Bohemia.

Periodically the lodge sponsors dances with Czech bands occasionally using some of the self-taught musicians among the membership. Music, a vital link to their culture, merits a Czech proverb, "He who is Czech, is a musician."

Frank and the family usually attend at least one dance a year held in the town hall. A night out dancing gives them the opportunity to socialize with a number of Bohemian families in the area. One such occasion excites a flurry of activity among the family in making themselves presentable for such an auspicious affair. After taking turns for baths in the tin tub and searching for their best attire, the family arrives at the hall to hear the lighthearted sounds of music streaming from the building. For an evening, they all can revisit their roots, not that they regret coming to America, but their heritage runs deep, threading its way through every fiber of their being.

"Look, Marie, my sister, Rosie and Adolf are here," says Frank as he approaches the couple that recently moved to Mullen from Spencer. Their conversation buzzes with talk of the impending marriage of brother Mike to a young woman, Katherine, a niece of an area homesteader.

Marie pulls Frank aside for a moment and motions for him to look on the dance floor. "Isn't that the young Klima girl

Albert is dancing with?" she asks Frank. "They make a fine looking couple."

"Soon all my brothers will be married and settled down," approves Frank.

"I'm going to visit with Mary Supik for awhile," she tells Frank as she moves away.

Marie sits down next to Mary and Joe. Marie and Mary know each other from the village of Mohelnice, Bohemia, where they were both born, Marie in 1881 and Mary in 1870. Mary left for America in 1892, and Marie did not see her again until they both finally settled near Dixon. They catch up on news from the Old Country.

After greeting the neighbors and relatives, Frank grasps Marie's arm and swirls her around the dance floor in a grace-ful tempo to a waltz, the two-step, and then a polka until Marie pleads for a rest as she is, again, in the family way.

The children reacquaint themselves with cousins they have not seen for awhile. The older ones practice dancing with each other and when they tire of that, they play with the younger children.

Late in the evening, after working up an appetite from dancing and visiting, they all help themselves to sausages, bread, and coffee. The men wash down their lunch with beer, *pivo*, while the women drink coffee. With tired children in their arms, they depart for home in the bright moonlit night.

In August, as Marie turns the handle on the barrel churn whipping the cream into butter, she tries to ignore the per-sistent pains tormenting her at regular intervals. Finally, no longer able to disregard them, she searches for a particular red cloth to hang on the clothesline to signal her sister-in-law Barbara for help. Since the men left early for the field and

*Mike and Katherine's Wedding portrait, 1908. Attendants: Albert and Agnes. Photo courtesy of Sharon Guthrie*

Charley, now six, has gone to visit his grandmother, she finds herself alone with the two younger children. She finishes up her churning while the red cloth flags the attention of Barbara, who arrives just in time to deliver Emil in 1909.

Within two years of Albert's arrival, Tripp County opens for settlement. Albert draws 160 acres of land near Hamill on which to file. He marries the young woman from the dance, Agnes, who is willing to share his life and his desire to build up a homestead. The children miss their young uncle with his dark, curly hair and mischievous eyes who likes to tease and teach them funny English words that he learned when he came to America at the age of fourteen.

᠁ ᠁ ᠁

Hot, dry winds blow from the south in the summer of 1910. Frank's corn and grain struggles due to lack of rain, then it withers in the wind.

"Looks like we are in for a long dry spell," says Marie as she closes the windows and door to the scorching hot wind, a certain messenger of drought.

"We will have to do the best we can this year. We can always hope that next year will be better," says Frank trying to not sound discouraged. "At least we aren't in debt, and we bought land relinquished by settlers who couldn't make it or were just looking for a fast profit when we had the money. We just have to hold on."

"We were just getting ahead. The past four years were good years and now this. Even with the good years we still have to scrimp and save. There is only money for the necessities." Marie finishes up the dishes, then takes the water in the dishpan and flings it outdoors on a struggling tree she has

*Albert and Agnes' wedding portrait, 1910.*
*Photo courtesy of Jim Beranek*

*Frank's parents Vaclav and Barbara.*

transplanted in the yard. She returns to the house rearranging her disheveled hair. "I think I got more water on my skirt than the tree," she says glancing down at her water spotted skirt. "This wind is terrible. Maybe the cattlemen are right. This land is better for cattle than for farming."

After the day of heat and wind, the sun retreats into the western horizon calming the wind on its descent. The earth seems to sigh with relief, grateful for the cool respite of the

*Seated: Marie and Barbara (Frank's mother). Standing: (second from left) Katherine and Barbara (Vaclav's Wife). Photo courtesy of Jim Beranek*

evening. The prairie grasses release a pungent sun baked perfume that drifts in the air. Once again the prairie becomes alive with sounds of chirping crickets, howling coyotes, and the mourning doves cooing their peaceful melody.

Mike and Katherine, now married and living on Mike's claim, become discontented due to their discouraging start. The alkaline water, unfit for humans or animals, kills the pigs and chickens that were given to them as a wedding present by neighbors and relatives. The drought does not lift their spirits either. After only two years on their homestead, they and their daughter leave for a neighboring county.

Drought continues to plague the land in 1911. The government begins to experiment with drought resistant grasses and forage crops. Even so, discouraged settlers leave, feeling that they have been misled into thinking that they would

*Standing: (second from the left) Vaclav, Albert, Frank and Mike.*
*Photo courtesy of Jim Beranek*

grow rich fast in this Promised Land. Abandoned home sites seem to cry out in disappointment.

In spite of hard times, Marie sorts through the wicker trunk for baby clothes. Another baby, William, becomes the youngest of five children.

Frank's parents also become disillusioned with this land and move near Hamill to live with Albert. They leave their little house in the draw, later to be moved by several teams of horses. The community of family dwindles.

In order to supplement their sparse income during these lean years, Frank takes a job unloading ferries at Landing Creek on the Missouri River. The notorious river carves its way across seven states transforming the landscape on a regular basis by obliterating islands, cutting bluffs, and moving the course of the river. The mighty river is a nightmare to navigators with its snags, sawyers, sandbars, collapsing embankments, and strong currents.

Frank and Marie, born too late to witness the early pirogues and keelboats of the fur trade era ply their way up the river, do see the last of steamboat traffic and become familiar with many of the landings established to accommodate the steamboats and their cargo.

Since the river divides South Dakota into the east and the west river country, ferries appeared out of necessity to transport people, livestock, and supplies from one bank to the other. Frank and Marie as well as other settlers living in this remote area take advantage of the ferry service. Living so far from towns, they load their wagons with flour, sugar, lumber and other items brought across on the ferries. Oftentimes, the supplies can be bought more cheaply this way.

Depending on which landing the traveler chooses, the construction of the ferry varies. Marie prefers the diesel-fueled paddle wheelers built in New Orleans. They seem safer to her than the flatboats propelled along with oars and tossed around at the whim of the river. But even those of crude construction can carry across a wagon or car as well as livestock.

Marie's occasional excursions, crossing the river on flat bottomed boats to visit neighboring towns to the east, become unnerving at times. The unpredictable river hurls obstacles in the path of the ferry without warning. The uncertain stability of the railings provides the only sense of security between her and the churning water, but her faith in Frank's swimming ability calms her fears a bit. But then, there remains the return trip. She and Frank can depart in the morning when the purring giant laps gently at the boat, but all can change in the afternoon when the fast changing

Dakota weather rolls up white caps on the water enough to still the courage of the most daring. On such trips as these, Marie vows she will stay home next time.

Marie watches during the drought years as the settlers in their loaded wagons, especially those from the drier lands farther west, pass by her claim retreating to the east. Their wagons bumble down the trail, oftentimes containing no more possessions than when they first came. Once they arrive at the ferry, Frank helps the fleeing homesteaders cross the river to the east at the Landing Creek Crossing. Their distraught, haggard faces take one more glance back at the land that defeated them before they cross to the other side.

After two years of drought and struggle to survive, Marie awakens to a light tapping on the window of the soddy. She springs out of bed to confirm that her ears aren't deceiving her. "Frank, it's raining. Come and see." She throws open the door and catches the glorious scent of the life giving moisture. She stands in the doorway for some time unable to tear her eyes away from a sight so long in coming.

The trees, grasses, and fields drink in the rain. Vibrant greens return to the land, bringing hope for better years

*Chapter Six*

# Expanding

With the advent of World War I, improving farm prices encourage greater production. Frank buys more land when he has the money and breaks it with the sulky, a horse drawn plow. He also leases land from the Indians living on the Rosebud.

The government, under the Allotment Act of the late 1880's, parceled out land to every enrolled tribal member to be used for farming or ranching in hopes that they would follow the example of the white population with land use and assimilate into white culture. Those that did not want to farm or ranch could lease their allotment, and even eventually sell it, after following certain restrictions from the Secretary of the Interior.

From his association with the Indians, Frank becomes their friend and learns to speak some Lakota. They often come to the place seeking a variety from their repetitious diet. They especially relish mature stewing hens. Marie obliges their wish to trade and catches several hens for their soup pot.

As the homesteaders expand by plowing up more land and building fences, they push the cattlemen back on lands unfit for cultivation along the Missouri River.

The cattlemen have occupied the area since the late 1800's leasing land on the Indian reservations to raise longhorns brought up from Texas, later to be sold to markets in the East. A portion of cattle was driven to the Indian agencies to supply beef to satisfy the treaty requirements of providing meat for the Indians. The cattlemen also supplied cattle to build up herds for the Indians living on their allotments as well as to local settlers who wanted to start small herds.

A cloud of dust billows up in the east during the spring of 1914. Marie looks long and hard. Her eyes routinely scan the horizon for smoke from prairie fires or wind and funnel formations from green, gray clouds. But this disturbance looks like neither. She hurries to find Frank.

Already sensing what she is going to ask, he explains, "I think that's the trail drive from the Mulehead Ranch Headquarters to the south of here. They are probably driving cattle to the Westonka, the north end of their large ranch. "Why don't we take the buckboard over there and have a look."

Grateful to get a break from her daily chores, she accepts Frank's invitation. "The older children can watch the younger ones for awhile," she tells Frank. "We won't be gone that long, will we?"

After several miles, they hear the bawling of the white-faced Hereford cattle, now replacing the longhorns, and shouts of the cowboys clad in western hats, chambray shirts, Levis, and chaps.

"I see the cowboys still wear their six-shooters just like they did when they first came to Dixon in the early days," says Marie.

"I guess they have to. Cattle rustling and horse thievery are such a problem, not to mention coyotes and wolves preying upon the weak cows and young calves. I hear a group of concerned settlers and town people are organizing a committee in Dixon to try and put a stop to the horse thieving around here."

"Maybe they will catch whoever stole our best horses the other night," says Marie, disgusted that someone would have the nerve to make off with something of theirs.

The Anti-Horse-Thief Association organizes in Dixon and pursues a group of horse thieves in the area, tracks them down, and makes an example of the identified crooks. This halts the horse stealing incidents for some time. However, the owners brand their horses for further protection from theft. Frank and Marie discover their horse thief proves to be the son of a settler in the region.

Frank continues to improve his homestead during the summer of the same year. As a result of their prosperity, Frank hauls lumber in from Gregory, a neighboring town located about twenty miles to the south. The railroad, completed through Gregory in 1907, now serves the surrounding communities, making markets and goods more available.

Marie, thrilled with the thought of finally having a real home, breathes in deeply of the fresh sawed lumber. Sod houses not meant to be permanent are prone to be damp, dark, and leaky during heavy rains. These rains threaten the cave in of the roof and walls. Marie walks through the skeleton framework of the house that the men have erected so far.

She imagines the rooms and how they will look, especially the large kitchen where she will spend so much of her time. Out of the smooth, fresh boards, a two-story house gradually emerges with two rooms downstairs, the kitchen and the living room, and two bedrooms upstairs. Still, there won't be enough room, but they will manage. Frank surprises her with a fancy stained glass window for her living room. "I saw the window and since you still don't have the big house you wanted, I thought the window would help make up for it," he says.

After several weeks of work, the house is finished and the cistern completed for water storage. They begin to move what little furniture they have from the soddy into the house.

"We need a new table and a bigger stove," says Marie with her hands on her hips, scanning the open space.

"Over time we can replace what we have with something better. The spring wheat looks good this year," says Frank.

"Children, off those stairs!" scolds Marie. "If they aren't playing on the stairs they are playing in the pantry under the stairs."

"It's something new to explore. They'll soon tire of the stairs. Let's have some music to celebrate. Frank, my boy, bring the accordion and I'll teach you all a new tune."

In the same year, Marie's mother receives title to her land. Since she no longer needs to live on her claim, she rejoins Marie in her new home, sleeping in the living room and caring for her brood of grandchildren including a new grandchild, Agnes. They move the shanty to Frank's place and use it for a tool shed.

In August, Marie scours the canyons for wild fruit. The tall grasses, mosquitoes, poison ivy, and snakes offer a deterrent to her success, but she doesn't give up.

"Frank, back the wagon up to those chokecherry bushes so I can stand in the wagon box and pick them without having to wade through the weeds," says Marie.

"Are you sure this is a good spot? Maybe that clump over there would be better," Frank motions towards another thicket.

"No, this will do." She steps up into the wagon and begins stripping the plump clusters of dark purple fruit into a bucket. Mosquitoes swarm and whine around her face. Between handfuls of berries she flails her arms around her head in vain to ward off the pesky creatures. The sun beats hot against her heavy clothes, wisps of hair drenched in sweat dangle about her face. She hurriedly sweeps them back with her hand. Berries that miss the bucket lay on the wagon bed mashed in a purple-blue hue. Stained fingers pull off yet more fruit.

"Pick a few red, less ripened berries. They help thicken the jelly when it's cooking," says Marie as she tastes some of the chokecherries.

Frank laughs at her puckering mouth, "What's the matter? Are they sour?"

"You wouldn't think that something that looks so good could taste so sour. But it makes wonderful tasting jelly on fresh baked bread smeared first with newly churned butter. I have more than enough here. Let's go. This brush is making me itch."

In another month the plums will also be ripe, provided the blossoms didn't freeze during the spring. Marie will again search the creek bottoms for the sweet wild plums for her fruit hungry family. Marie misses the cherry and the plum trees that grew so profusely in Bohemia. The wild fruit on the prairie does not compare with the easily obtainable fruit in the Old Country. Nor do wild plums work for her plum dumplings smothered in sugar, cinnamon, butter, and cream.

As the wagon pulls up out of the draw, Marie spots greenish flowers twining around a tree. "Stop the wagon. I think I see wild hops over there." After the wagon comes to a halt, she jumps down and gathers the cone shaped flowers cascading from the vine. Although the hops are used primarily for beer making, when they are dried she can use them as a leavening agent to raise her bread. On their way home, Marie keeps a sharp eye out for other growing herbs and plants useful for teas, poultices, as well as other healing agents. Settlers and Indians share their knowledge of native plants to keep their families healthy.

Hot days mellow into approaching fall. Fruits ripen and vegetables mature in Marie's garden.

"Some of the cabbage are cracking," says Marie returning from the garden one morning. She enjoys the daily ritual of watching the progress of each growing thing. But more important, survival and livelihood depend on the success of the harvest.

"This is as good a time as any to make kraut," says Marie's mother reaching for the kraut cutter and the teakettle of scalding water.

"Boys, bring up the big crock from the cellar so I can wash it and get it ready for the shredded cabbage," says Marie as she goes back to the garden to lug in the heads of cabbage.

"I'll strip the outer leaves, wash them up, and core them when you bring them in, then you can begin shredding," says

Marie's mother as she pulls up her sleeves to ready herself for the task.

Marie takes the washed cabbage and places it in the wooden boxed frame, which slides in the grooves of the long kraut cutter, just the right size for a firm head of cabbage. She moves the wooden frame containing the cabbage over sharp blades, shredding it into thin, light green crisp ribbons. A pan underneath catches the shredded pieces. When the pan is full, Marie's mother empties it into the crock, adds salt, and stomps it down with a wooden plunger to bring out the juices ensuring that it will work and ferment. Soon fragments of the vegetable cover the table.

"Save the larger pieces that we don't use for the sauerkraut, and we will use them for dinner, says Marie to her mother. "Sweet and sour cabbage with the pork I have left will taste good."

"That's strange. Frank's coming toward the house carrying his hat," says Marie's mother glancing through the window as she wipes up the final traces of cabbage.

"I'll go and see what he is up to," says Marie anxious to get out of the house and get some fresh air. "What do you have there in your hat?" she says mopping up the perspiration from her face with her apron.

The sun glistens on the sandy hair of his hatless head. "I found some wild grapes down along the river, and I thought they would make some fine wine. You know, a good winter tonic," he says, holding up a cluster of dark purple grapes to admire.

"You and your tonic," laughs Marie. "There should be another crock in the cellar for your grapes, but be careful where you dump the leavings from you wine. Remember last year? The chickens got into it and were a bit woozy for a few days."

*Chapter Seven*

# Sorrow and Healing

The family gathers in the wind swept Bull Creek Cemetery outside of Dixon in 1916 to lay *Babicka*, Marie's mother, to rest. The familiar buttes, iced in snow when she first came to this new land, pose as sentinels to watch over her for all eternity. The family feels a void in their lives, especially Marie. She will miss the companionship, the motherly advice, and the one who made living out here so much easier, who cared for her children as if they were her own. But a baby boy, Vincent, born the same year keeps her busy, now bringing the total number of children to seven.

❦ ❦ ❦

An airborne phantom sweeps through America in 1918 leaving a path of pain, heartache, fear, suffering, and death in one year's time. Its insatiable appetite propels it through Europe, Asia, and the entire world leaving millions dead. The phantom isn't selective. It steals the young, the old, the poor, the rich, the strong, or the weak. No one knows when the scourge will strike, and worst of all there is no protection from it. The heartless intruder consumes mothers and daughter, fathers and sons; sometimes even the entire family healthy only twelve hours before, now already a memory. During the winter, the Spanish Influenza visits the home of Frank and Marie.

Marie moves through the kitchen slowly, methodically, weak from past days of high fever and delirium. She dips into a crock of sauerkraut fermenting behind the stove, skims off the white scum formed on top, and takes out a heaping portion of kraut. Then she places it in a black cast iron skillet to fry. Her family lies sick, suffering from the effects of the Spanish Influenza.

The sickness begins with a fever, sore throat, headache, and muscle aches. She knows it can develop into pneumonia, a horrible never seen before kind, that turns people blue and black. The lungs swell with fluid and then collapse killing the sufferer. She does her best to keep her family from succumbing to the disease.

Appetites wane with the sickness. Sauerkraut seems like the only thing that anyone will eat. She dishes it up and distributes it to those able to eat, then she sits down at the table and forces a forkful in her mouth. She hears Frank pull up outside the door and sees that his arms are full of bundles.

"Open the door quick! I'm about to drop these packages," shouts Frank.

She opens the door and relieves him of several packages, cold to the touch from the winter air.

"My hands feel so frozen that I can't hang on to anything. My what a miserably cold winter we are having."

Even though the family keeps themselves isolated to avoid spreading the dreaded disease, Frank, still recovering from the flu, makes a trip to Dixon to get supplies as well as information.

"What did you find out in town?" Marie eagerly asks.

"There is still nothing you can do for the influenza, even the vaccines they developed don't work. But they are saying the influenza is dying out in the East. We seem to be one of the last areas hit."

"Since there is nothing else we can do, I'll just continue with my home remedies," she says as she assembles the ingredients for another batch of mustard plaster, believed to loosen congestion when applied to the chest. She mixes powdered mustard, flour, water, and vinegar to make stiff dough. She then places it in a cloth and takes several swift stitches sewing it up so the mixture won't leak out. "My father died of influenza in the Old Country, but it was nothing like this." She climbs the stairs to apply the mustard plaster to a sick child.

Miraculously, the family recovers, whether due to an immunity or to Marie's home remedies. However, all is not well. Frank receives word in late December that his younger brother, Albert in Hamill, has died from the influenza at the age of thirty.

"It's too cold for you to make a trip to Hamill in this weather with a team and wagon," says Marie in a distressed voice. "You haven't fully recovered yourself."

"I have to go. Don't worry. Vac will go with me. With the weather as bad as it is, not too many will be there to offer comfort."

"Albert leaves a wife and young children. I wonder what Agnes will do now." Marie picks up Edward, the newest addition to the family, and holds him close.

"Vac and I will be gone several days. Don't worry. There are homesteads along the way where we can warm ourselves if we have to. Do you think you can put a patch on this heavy coat of mine before I leave?" asks Frank.

The next morning, Frank hitches up his team, hunched against the cold in spite of their shaggy winter hair. Marie follows Frank outside to see him off, shuddering as winter's icy fingers creep along her spine. She makes sure the gunnysack with heated bricks rests at his feet before she returns to the house.

Once again she watches him leave her alone out on the frozen prairie. Frank's last departing farewell freezes in the frigid air.

⚜ ⚜ ⚜

The spring brings forth the rebirth of promise for better days, the healing sun, and fresh vivifying air for those recovering from the ravages of the winter. The buds of the wild rose bush open in abundance along the creek banks. The delicate pink flowers dispatch a sweet fragrance romancing the breeze as it drifts across the land.

In days back, Spotted Tail and his folk named a creek the Rosebud because of the profusion of wild roses along its banks. The Rosebud, more than a name to the Lakota, became a symbol to the joy of beauty found in the landscape. And with that joy, they believed, Mother Earth sang songs through every living thing, including the wild rose.

Later the Indian agency, a steamboat landing, a steamboat, a bridge, and the land where the homesteaders settled in Gregory County adopt the name the Rosebud. This spring the land lives up to its name.

At Albert's grave site at the Roseland Cemetery. Hamill. Photo courtesy of Jim Beranek

In spite of the gay sunshine, fragrant flowers, and warmer weather, Marie, pale and listless, has difficulty bouncing back from the troublesome winter.

"What you need is a good long hike through the river hills. You've been wanting to dig up some cedar trees and transplant them around the yard. Why don't we just do that today before the weather becomes too hot?" says Frank.

"Maybe you're right. Everything seems like such drudgery for me lately," admits Marie.

Dainty purple violets bloom on the moisture soaked hill-sides while they search up and down the draws for small cedars that will survive being moved.

"Try to get all the root with it," Marie tells him as she places the dug cedars in the wagon.

Tired, yet exhilarated, from tramping through the canyons, they decide they have dug enough and start for home.

"Plant one by the house here," she says when they get back, lifting a cedar out of the wagon.

"I won't be able to see out the window. The tree will be in the way," protests Frank.

"Oh, it will years before the tree gets that tall."

"Well, alright, then, get some water and dump it in this hole," Frank relents, happy to see that Marie seems like her old self.

Due to dry conditions in Western South Dakota, more settlers retreat to the East. But the Dixon community enjoys good years in 1918 and 1919. Frank and Marie take advantage of the good weather in their area. They practice diversified farming by planting a variety of crops such as corn, alfalfa, and feed grains. They also raise livestock, even before the encouragement of the government to diversify farming to try and offset the discouraging farming experiences of the past. They are one step ahead of the advice because they learned diversified farming in Bohemia. But with diversification comes the expense of added equipment, added livestock, and the expansion of larger land holdings, which results in mortgaged farms for most. Even with favorable weather conditions, efficient farming practices, and the emergence of drought resistant grains and alfalfa, the fickle rising and falling farm prices for their commodities and the high cost of machinery make farming a challenge.

In 1920, when Marie turns 39, her namesake joins the family with the birth of the ninth child. The couple buries a premature daughter born a few years afterwards, her last pregnancy, in the grove of trees behind the house in a coffin made by her father. No longer encumbered with child bearing, Marie finds she possesses a newfound vitality.

ᴎᴈ ᴎᴈ ᴎᴈ

Marie breathes in deeply of the invigorating spring fresh prairie air. The sweet fragrance of blooming Russian olives, planted as part of a windbreak to help stop the sweep of the north wind, wafts on the morning breeze. The windbreak provides shelter for wildlife and shade for Marie's chickens. No matter how long she has lived here, she finds the wind, *vitr*, difficult to get use to, so different from Bohemia.

Marie, always ready to greet the day at first light, expects everyone else to do the same. She yells up the stairs at 5:30 AM, "Frank, get out of bed. The neighbors are already in the fields." There's work to be done. Everyone must be up.

She braids her long hair and winds it up into a tight bun at the back of her head. Then, she prepares a breakfast of oatmeal and coffee. Satisfied that everyone is up and on task, she dons her scarf and ventures outside to do her morning chores.

A mother hen clucks raucously to a little brood of chicks faithfully following behind. The hen scratches the ground, calling her chicks over for a tasty morsel she has found. One chick gets in her way of the vigorous scratching and tumbles head over feet. Unhurt, he jumps up and partakes of a morning snack.

About a month ago, Marie set a cluck on twelve eggs; where undisturbed the broody hen could keep her eggs warm and safe. Occasionally the hen would get off her nest and run for a little feed and water but always faithfully returned. In about three weeks, the chicks pecked through the brittle shell and emerged wet and wobbly. In a short time, they dried into a fluff ball, gained their land legs, and were ready to go on an excursion with their agitated mother.

Being so small, the chicks are vulnerable to practically anything. If something looks likely to harm her chicks, the old hen ruffles her feathers and takes chase. Elements beyond the hen's control, such as hailstorms, threaten her chicks, requiring Marie's assistance in chasing the chickens to safety when clouds look menacing.

This morning, Marie scatters grain on the ground to make finding breakfast a little easier. When grown, the young pullets will provide eggs for cooking. The roosters will make good fryers.

She inspects the garden and potato patch after tending the chickens, choosing the cool of the day for pulling and hoeing pesky weeds. She reaches down, gives the weeds several twists, and pulls them from the ground so that the root no longer is able to grow deep in search for water. A close look at the potato patch reveals a striped potato bug foraging on the tender young leaves. A flick of the finger discards the voracious bugs into a can for disposal at a later time. Without prompt removal of the bugs, the plant will be reduced to sticks, and no potatoes will be dug in the fall. The potato, *brambory*, was an essential food in the Old Country as it is here. A day hardly goes by that she doesn't cook something using potatoes, whether it is boiled potatoes, potato dumplings, potato pancakes, potato soup, fried potatoes, or potato bread.

She looks at the sun almost straight up in the sky. Her family will be gathering for dinner shortly. She would rather remain outdoors, but she needs to prepare the noon meal.

A soft prairie breeze flutters the curtains in the east window cooling the kitchen. A long wooden table with a full-length bench extends across the east side of the room near the window. In the center of the table, a cut glass spoon holder contains spoons; handle side down in wait to stir the coffee. A white cupboard trimmed in red takes up a corner near the north wall containing many interesting sized drawers, some holding silverware and other items. Coffee cups hang on hooks, and peppermint candy is tucked away amidst the neatly stacked dishes. Another cupboard on the opposite wall displays hand painted bone china cups and saucers, premiums or gifts given upon the purchase of staples such as flour, coffee beans, or oatmeal. The brightly painted pink and lavender flowered gold-rimmed dishes offer a sharp contrast to her simple life.

Marie busily scrapes potatoes with a sharp spoon for today's dinner. Being a frugal woman, she believes in conserving every morsel of food. Part of a pot of uneaten oatmeal sits on the stove from breakfast. With the proper ingredients and a handful of raisins, it will bake up into delectable cookies to go with the afternoon coffee.

The family fills the kitchen looking forward to one of her meals, usually a simple but filling dish. Her specialties include sauerkraut and dumplings, referred to as *knedlecky* in Bohemian, and various soups, and potato dishes. Much to the chagrin of her son Vincent, a T-bone steak often ends up in the soup pot. She has no time for pie baking, but she makes light and tasty donuts with plenty of strong dark coffee to wash them down.

The meal often ends in a political debate between Marie and her son Charley. She, like most of her country folk who emigrated from Bohemia, can read and write in her native tongue. Marie, well read with the many Czech newspapers and periodicals published in America that represents many different viewpoints, subscribes to at least one publication. She seldom agrees with everything written and likes to wrangle the issues with Charley who also verses himself on current affairs.

"But, Ma, it's not like that here," he often counters in exasperation.

The vocal family, each with definite opinions, debate and argue over almost everything, often disrupting the household.

After putting the kitchen back in order after dinner, Marie takes her patching and retires to the cool living room. With six sons and a husband, an endless amount of patching awaits her. Even the underwear gets patches if need be. A soft breeze murmurs peacefully in the quiet afternoon. She grows weary from the long day she has put in and nods off in a short catnap. Eventually, she awakens with a start and drowsily finishes up her final stitches, folds the patching, giving it a soft caress she lays it on the table.

She makes another trip to the hen house to gather the eggs and give the chickens fresh water. Then it is time for the afternoon coffee, *kava*. In the late afternoon, the family gathers for coffee and the cookies that Marie baked this morning. The small repast fortifies them all for several more hours of daylight, too precious to idle away.

"Where's young Frank?" says Marie, noticing that he is not among the rest.

"The last time I saw him he was headed out to check the fence line in the south pasture," says Emil. "He should have been back by now."

"If he doesn't come in by supper time, I want you boys to go and look for him," she says with concern in her voice.

Mealtime comes and goes and there's still no sign of young Frank. She sends Emil and William to look for him. She puts young Frank's supper in the warming oven above the stove for his return. About forty-five minutes later they return bringing Frank into the house dazed.

"Where did you find him? What happened? Marie says hurrying over to him.

"We found him on the ground, delirious, thrown from his horse," says William. "It took awhile to find his horse, or we would have been back sooner."

"Help him over to the chair. We had better watch him for awhile." She fusses over him until she's assured he's alright.

Her protective instinct and her need to know their whereabouts at all times forms a strong bond with her sons even into adulthood.

Several weeks later as she hangs her wash out on the clothesline, she notices Frank and the boys leading a half-starved horse behind the wagon. "Where did you find that skinny horse? You can count its ribs." Astonished with the condition of the poor animal, she strokes his drooping head.

"The boys found him tied to a tree while we were looking for cedar posts down by the river. A fellow's boots and clothes were strewn all around. He must have gone in for a swim and drowned instead," says Frank.

*South Dakota, 1920.*

"I'm always warning you boys to be careful of the treacherous current in that river when you go down there fishing, and I'm sure you try to sneak in a swim," she says to her sons. "Whoever his kin is will never know what happened to him."

"Boys take the horse away and give him some feed, but don't let him over eat. No arguing on who gets the horse."

"The way you all love horses, you'll have that poor beast in fine shape in no time," says Marie.

*Chapter Eight*

# Harvest

"How about going with me to check the wheat?" asks Frank taking a long drink from the dipper out of the water pail in the kitchen. "I'm sure you would like to get out of this hot kitchen."

"Wait just a minute. Let me finish up these beans." After removing the jars filled with beans from the canner of hot water and covering them with a dishtowel, she grabs her scarf and walks with Frank to the field.

The couple looks with amazement on the waving golden fields. "Well, we've made it this far without any devastating hail," says Frank as he stops to break off a head of wheat. In the palm of his hand, he separates the berries from the hull, takes out a kernel, and pops it in his mouth to test the hardness of the grain. "I think we should be able to bring the binder to the field and begin the harvest in a few days." They both glance at the sky toward the western horizon to check their optimism for a bountiful yield.

Frank sharpens the binder sickle on a large grindstone wheel driven by a foot pedal. The boys grease the moving parts of the binder and check the canvas. On a hot day in July, they hitch three horses to the binder, the weakest horse to the outside, and begin to cut the ripened grain. The rotating wooden reel slats of the binder move through the field like a side paddle wheeler on the river, drawing the grain into the moving sickle powered by the drive wheel. The machine sizes the cut grain into a bundle, ties it with twine, and kicks it into the bundle carrier. Maneuvering a lever, Frank drops three to four bundles adjacent to the piles left on the previous round forming windrows. The boys use pitchforks to avoid getting bitten by a rattler hiding under the sheaves, to stand two bundles upright balanced against each other. Then, they prop up two more from either side to form a shock. They adjoin more bundles, checking to see that the drying air can circulate through the bound grain. The number of bundles required to form a shock depends on how long it will remain in the field before threshing. Since it will be some time before the threshing rig will arrive at their place, they decide on an eight-bundle shock. Marie, not wanting to be left out of the harvest, wields a cumbersome pitchfork, which she soon abandons to add another bundle. Young Frank tosses up the ninth bundle capping off the shock to protect it from rain. At noon, the working crew unhitches the horses to be turned out in the pasture to be replaced later by a fresh team of horses. After caring for the horses, they head for the house where the girls have dinner waiting for them. Hot and dusty, they leave the field that is beginning to fill with golden pyramids of grain. After the meal and a little rest, the men return to the field to continue the harvest provided the grain isn't to dry to bind. Marie decides to remain at the house during the heat of the day.

Frank does not own his own threshing machine yet, so he has to wait for the hired rig and crew to make the rounds in the neighborhood. Finally, they arrive with the monstrous machine ready to separate the kernels of grain from the stalk. Neighbors and relatives living nearby bring their teams and hayracks to help with the work. Upon their arrival, they begin to pitch the shocked bundles into the hayracks. When the men load the hayracks, the horses bring them up to the clattering threshing machine. The team shies a bit from the thundering noise of the machine, but brought under control by the men, they pull up along side of the thresher where the men pitch off bundles into the feeder headfirst. The golden straw comes flying out of a long metal neck along with chaff and dust. Several unlucky men have the job of building the straw pile. By the time they finish, chaff and dust cover them. The separated grain pours out of a spout collected in an awaiting wagon.

While the men toil in the grain field, the women swelter in the kitchen preparing a meal for the threshing crew.

Marie tosses a few more corncobs into her wood cook stove, making for a very fast, hot fire. Earlier this morning she dressed chickens now ready for the frying pan. She places the floured chicken pieces in the sizzling grease, and then turns her attention to the garden produce she picked early this morning. The neighbor women, who have come to help, peel the potatoes.

The radiating heat of the stove turns the kitchen into a hot inferno. Occasionally, Marie turns to swat an intrusive fly ever present during harvest time. She places her hand in the hot oven to check the oven temperature. Just right, she concludes. She shoves a pan of buns in the oven to bake. She will need these for sandwiches for late afternoon lunch.

The aroma of golden fried chicken and freshly baked bread tantalize the appetites of the hot dusty men as they approach the house for the noon meal. After caring for their horses, the men wash off the itching chaff, dust, and sweat from their faces and hands using the washbasin, soap, and towels, which have been placed outside for their use. A few of the men relax in the shade by the tree while waiting for the final call to dinner.

The mounds of food disappear rapidly as the ravenous threshers replenish their energy by eating their way through mounds of fluffy potatoes dripping in white gravy, crunchy fried chicken, fresh vegetables and warm, buttered bread.

When the men finish, the women eat, taking their time to steal a little rest. A myriad of pots, pans, and skillets wait to be scoured in addition to the rest of the dishes. After many teakettles of hot water and several changes of the dirty dishwater, the women finally complete the task. The neighbor ladies depart to their own homes to do the afternoon chores. There's a little time left to gather the eggs before Marie makes donuts and sandwiches for the late afternoon meal. She puts the girls to work making sandwiches while she places a large gray graniteware coffee pot on the stove to boil. Then she fries the donuts. She packs up the lunch, sorts out the cups, stuffs a cloth into the spout of the coffee pot, and sends the girls to the field to feed the hungry crew. Finally, she gives a sigh to the long day and knows that it will be repeated several more days until threshing is over.

When the threshing is completed, Frank turns his thoughts to the corn crop. Because more acres are in production, Frank planted the field this spring with a lister, a type of horse drawn corn planter. He fills in the missing places with a hand planter. When Marie sees Frank on the way to the cornfield today, she takes a break from her chores and joins him. She likes to listen to the rustling sound of the corn as she walks down the tall rows. The corn plants stand sturdy, shiny and green, the leaves curled lightly to retain moisture. The two of them escape the shimmering heat waves and enter the cool shade of the cornfield's rustling leaves towering above them. Frank peels back the soft green husk and examines the ears to see how they are filling. He takes out a pocketknife and hacks off the black, rubbery corn smut threatening the corn plant. He digs down into the soft cultivated soil near the root using his pliers' handle and presses the dirt into a ball. "There's still good moisture yet," he says to Marie as he hands her the compressed soil. Lost in thought among the cornrows, they marvel at this new land.

To prepare for the corn harvest this fall, Frank shouts verbal commands to his team of horses as they ease the wooden wagon, needed for the harvest, into a water hole. "Back up Billie and Blackie, back, back," he says as he pulls on the reins. Frank leaves the wagon in the water for several weeks to tighten the drying spokes of the wheels so they will not come loose.

The sun begins its autumnal equinox by sliding to the south, marking the passing of another season. The nights become cooler as the days shorten. Golden and russet leaves fall from trees in the passing wind. The earth soaks up the last warmth in preparation for its winter slumber.

High above the cornfield, geese wing their way south. Their honking sound breaks in the cold morning air. Frank and the boys get ready to pick the mature corn by hand. This is considered to be one of the toughest jobs on the farm. They wear gloves to protect their hands from the sharp husks and rough corn, but they still suffer from the chaffing effects of the job as well as the cold morning air.

Marie hurries out to the cornfield with the dry change of gloves they forgot to take with them. She tarries awhile before she returns to her work. Frank and the boys strap on a device with a hook that can be worn over the glove to assist in stripping the husk from an ear of corn.

"Giddy up, Clyde and Zeke, giddy up," shouts Ed as the horses move down the row by themselves responding to the curt commands. Shortly, the thud of corn hits the high bang board, a temporary addition to one side of the wagon to keep the corn from being thrown over the side. Marie notices the boys skillfully tossing the corn into the wagon without looking up. She pitches in a few herself before she leaves.

When Frank isn't looking, the boys pelt each other with corn until he admonishes them to get back to work. The horse drawn wagon ambles down the field while the corn pickers continue the backbreaking labor. After a morning's work, the boys return to the place and shovel corn off the filled wagons into corncribs constructed of boards laid across posts for the floor and high open wire for the sides. With the crisp, click of the shovel, they empty the wagons into the crib where the corn will be stored until needed. A hearty meal and a short rest revive them for another round of corn picking.

When they finish the corn picking, Frank organizes his family for a wood cutting trip to the Missouri River. The undercut riverbanks and the constant flooding of the river uproots trees and sends them floating eventually to rest on the shore. These smooth white sun bleached remnants of the cottonwood trees line the bank making for excellent fire-wood in the cold winter months. Marie packs a lunch for the long day at the river.

The team and wagon pass by *Babicka's* old homestead as they make the three-mile trip to the river. The yellow-fringed brown faces of the sunflowers wave in the breeze nodding their heads in greeting. Before the steep descent to the river bottom, a vista of the river stretches out before them. The main channel winds itself to the northeast. Landing Creek, a small inlet, drops back and extends to the south where they will cut the wood.

The water laps against the shore churning white foam. Young Frank and Emil, the fishermen of the family, jump out of the wagon anxious to throw in their fishing lines in hopes of catching carp or catfish. Fried crisp and golden brown, the freshly caught fish will offer a change to tonight's supper.

"Boys, stick your poles in the mud. We came down here to cut wood," says Frank in a firm voice.

The boys reluctantly take the cross cut saws from the wagon. Pairing up, they commence the rhythm of the pulling motion of the lengthy saw careful not to buckle the metal tooth blade. After a time, little mounds of light saw dust build on the ground, evidence of progress. During the lunch break, they check their poles and find, to their delight, that they have caught a couple of fish.

During the afternoon, they cut more big logs into chucks for the stoves. The loaded wagon can hold no more. After retrieving their poles and enough fish for supper, the family finds a spot in the buckboard brought along for their trip back. The horses strain pulling the wagon against the heavy load of wood as they ascend the steep hills. Simultaneously, a flaming orange moon graces the horizon with its splendid glow. By the time the horses reach the plain, the full harvest moon in all its glory reaches towards its zenith illuminating their journey home.

*Chapter Nine*

# Winter

The family cuts the wood just in time. In the following week, a cold fierce wind blows out of the north carrying particles of snow in its icy breath. Marie throws on another log and stokes up the fire in order to heat the drafty house. The wind whistles through the windows and crawls under the doors sending a chill over the house. Flatirons warm on the stove, later to be wrapped in a heavy cloth and be placed in bed to warm the occupants. A register in the ceiling above the stove allows heat to reach upward to the upstairs bedrooms, but it's not enough to make the rooms comfortably warm. The children trudge up the winding stairs with wrapped flatirons in hand. They hurriedly exchange their day clothes for night-clothes and jump into bed under the bulky feather ticks. The more children the cozier as several pile into a single bed, burrowing under the covers to sleep snugly through the Arctic blast swirling around the house. They will have sweet dreams until morning when they have to face the frigid temperatures and wade through the deep snow first to do the daily chores and then on to school. Maybe there will be time to go sledding with the wooden runner sled after school.

The wind wails down the chimney. Logs pop and snap in the glowing stove. Wind and snow continually beat against the house. Marie turns the wick up on the kerosene lamp, lays her Bohemian papers out on the table, hands one to Frank, and begins to read. After the clamor of the day, there's a little time left for her. She pulls her chair closer to the stove. A teakettle softly sings in response to the screaming wind. After a time, the low flicker of a dwindling fire indicates the end to a winter evening.

The early light of the next morning filters through chilled windows glazed in a frosty mosaic of lace. The stiff, cold house creaks and groans from the battle with the wind. The night fire in the stove glows faintly, unable to ward off the subzero temperature from creeping in. The clang of a stove lid ensures that someone has dared to brave the bristling cold to build a roaring fire to warm the house. Marie breaks ice that has built up overnight in the water bucket with a sharp strike of the metal dipper. She pours the icy water into the coffee pot and grinds the coffee beans in the grinder. After several turns of the handle, the beans yield fragrant grounds. Shortly, the aroma of dark rich coffee steals up the stairway. Sleepyheads leave their warm nests to venture forth for a new day. Bare feet hit the cold floor sending shivers through the body. A gasp of warm breath hangs in the air. Hands grab chilled, lifeless clothes and in a flurry of activity everyone dresses.

After a breakfast of coffee and hardtack, a firm biscuit, the children tend to their morning chores. They pull gunnysacks over their shoes and tie them on with wire or twine. The rough sacks offer some protection to their feet during their chores and the walk to school through the deep snow that has drifted overnight.

Marie follows the children outside with a warm bucket of water for her chickens. She keeps an eye on her children as they scramble off to school, over a mile away.

Leaden skies hover in absolute stillness as the children struggle through the crunching snow with the awkward gunnysacks hindering their steps. Agnes and sister Marie gaily swing the lunch pail containing their noon meal of hardtack left over from breakfast, and lard, a substitute for butter.

A fresh slate of snow blankets the fields and pastures, marred here and there by rabbit and coyote tracks. The deer crisscross paths indicating an early morning revelry of wildlife. The children anxiously explore this fresh new world and leave their footprints as well. Vincent scoops up a handful of compressed snow and hurls it at brother Ed. The snowball hits its target and explodes into white powder. Laughter and scuffling follow each new attack.

The new school, recently built to replace the homestead shack that had served as the school in earlier years, accommodates as many as twenty-eight in attendance because of large families in the area. The school term consists of three months in the spring and three months in the winter. Even though the homesteaders realize the importance of education, they often keep their offspring at home to help with the abundant work. Because of demands on their time, some children do not even finish the eighth grade.

Marie's oldest sons, Charley, Frank, Emil, and Bill (William) remain at home since they have finished school. Anna now works in Gregory. During their spare moments, the older siblings teach their younger brothers and sisters English to help with the transition to school.

The children's newly learned English is not often up to standard and incurs reprimands from some of the teachers. The students occasionally retaliate by playing pranks on the teacher. Not sure if her children participate, Marie warns them about proper behavior. She reminds them of the challenging task of the teachers which is to teach the students English as well as the three R's. In addition, the headmaster must teach all eight grades with few books and supplies.

In spite of her warning, she hears stories in the neighborhood of students locking the teacher in the coal shed, or a particularly messy one when horse droppings were spread throughout the teacher's desk drawers. She shakes her head in her musing. When the older children attended school, they also brought home stories of ornery students using the flag for a horse blanket or tying a fellow classmate to a horse so he wouldn't get bucked off. There always seem to be some rambunctious older boys in the group to lead the rest astray.

After a break in the weather, Frank and the boys butcher a hog that Frank has traded from one of the neighbors. Because of the alkali in the soil on his place, he cannot raise pigs successfully. The pigs lose their hair and even eventually their hooves.

In the meantime, Marie boils large kettles of water on the stove to scald the butchered hog. The boys hurriedly lug the boiling water outside to the barn and dump it into a wooden barrel. In order to loosen the bristles, Frank lowers the hanging carcass from the barn rafters into the barrel of hot water to be scalded. He then lifts it out again to be scraped and skinned.

"Bring the hog's head in as soon as it has cooled," says Marie as she readies another kettle of water in which to cook the head, the tongue, and the liver. Several hours later, she strips the cooked meat off the head, lets it cool, and grinds it along with the tongue and the liver. She then breaks up dried bread, mixes it with the ground meat and adds salt, pepper, marjoram, and garlic. Frank attempts to snitch a piece of the boiled meat. Marie gently slaps him on the hand. "We need it all," she says. She elicits help from her family to fill the casing, made from the cleaned intestines of the hog, using the sausage stuffer. The meat mixture oozes from the stuffer into the casings. Marie ties off the casings, forming a ring, which she adds to a large pan already filling with *Jitrnice*, a Bohemian sausage.

"Ma, cook some for supper," the children beg.

She knows how much they like this tasty treat so she places a couple of rings in a skillet and places them in the oven. Soon the *Jitrnice* emerges from the oven sizzling and brown. Potatoes and sauerkraut, *zeli*, offer the perfect accompaniment to this Bohemian specialty.

The next day she continues the preserving process. Frank brings in a section of near frozen meat and saws off chops and steaks for Marie to prepare. She lays the slices in big black pans and places them in the oven to fry. Using butcher knives, they trim the lard from the hog, cut it into cubes, and dump it into a large cast iron pot to render. Soon, the greasy lard bubbles on the stove leaving cracklings floating on top, which she skims off into a colander and allows to drain.

The aroma of frying pork and the heavy scent of lard permeate the kitchen. She takes some of the fried pork out of the pan for supper, the rest she stores in crocks and covers with lard sealing it from the air. This process preserves the pork for a long time provided it is stored in a cool place.

She wastes very little of the butchered pig. She even uses the pig's knuckles near the pig's feet. Daughter Marie wrinkles her nose at the thought of this. "You are really going to eat these?" she says.

"They will taste pretty good when there is nothing else to eat," Marie says in a matter of fact tone. "Here, grind these cracklings, and I'll stir up something you like." After thoroughly washing the knuckles and cooking them, Marie makes a brine of vinegar, sugar, salt, pepper, and spices. She pours the pickling brine over the odd looking morsels layered in a glass jar and stores it in a cool place. She then mixes the ground cracklings with flour, milk, and salt, rolls them round and flat, and bakes them in the oven until crisp and lightly browned.

The butchered and preserved meat will not last long, but she will dole it out sparingly throughout the winter.

ꝏ ꝏ ꝏ

Several winters later as Marie gathers snow in wash tubs to melt, she glances up to see the boys and their dogs returning from a late afternoon tramp through the snow glazed hills to check the trap line. Ghost-like barren trees that line the creek bottoms look after them, beseeching the venturers with ragged gray arms. The boys draw closer with their catch of several days.

"How was your luck?" Marie asks stopping her task for a moment.

"We did alright, although the coyotes seem a bit mangy this winter," says young Frank.

The dogs tussle with each other before they scoot under the shed to rest after their long walk along the trap lines.

Marie follows her sons into the tool shed. The boys deposit their treasures on benches while hanging others on the wall in preparation for skinning. Marie can't help but run her hands through the thick winter fur of the masked raccoons and beaver.

"Someone back East will enjoy a fine coat made out of these furs," she says imagining what one would look like on her.

"I just hope the fur buyer will give us a good price," says Emil admiring his catch of rabbits.

"Skin the snared rabbits quickly, and I'll fry them for supper," she says as she leaves to fill up the tubs. As an afterthought she adds, "One of you boys can carry in the snow for me."

Later that evening, the quietness of another long winter night enfolds the house. All the trapping stories have been told and retold. Young Frank and Charley have just finished cutting each other's hair. With no one else needing a haircut, they look for something to pass time.

"Let's practice our music, just in case we are asked to play for another dance," suggests Vincent. In keeping with family tradition, the talented musicians in the family occasionally play for dances held in newly built barns, homes, or remote dance halls. Quiet and forlorn, the halls frown in neglect until Saturday night when the hills resound with music, laughter, and the quickened step of folks looking forward to an evening's entertainment.

Liking Vincent's idea, the rest of the family grab kitchen chairs and place them in a semi-circle in the living room.

Since most members of the family can play more than one instrument, they decide who will play what for the evening. Young Frank takes up his trumpet, Vincent the Jew's harp, Bill and Emil the accordions, Ed the harmonica, and sister Marie the guitar. "I'll sit this one out," says Frank, already keeping time to the music with his tapping foot. The living room, a miniature Carnegie Hall for a night, returns to nostalgic ethnic roots. With music, the family keeps their heritage and culture alive as well as lessen the cares of the work worn day.

Strains of music drift from the frame house out into the star-filled night. The austere cold lines of the landscape seem to soften as waltzes glide across the snow covered plains.

Marie listens to the old familiar songs and joins in the singing. A vision of green rolling hills, castles, cobbled stone streets, colorful embroidered native costumes, *kroj*, and folk dancing of her native country flash through her mind. Briefly a twinge of homesickness tugs at her heart, but she looks upon Frank and their family with no regrets.

*Chapter Ten*

# Quiet Voices

A meadowlark sings his cheerful song banishing the cold dismal winter. The new spring looks promising. During the last few years, crops thrived with abundant moisture, but farm prices severely dropped causing an agricultural depression. Expansion loans granted to the farmers during World War I cannot be paid, and banks fail. Dry years return progressing to a severe drought in 1929, the year of the stock market crash.

Frank and Marie can hardly believe their eyes when the first cloud of grasshoppers driven by the wind descends on their place in 1933, depositing thousands of grasshoppers on their land. The destructive insects chew their way through any vegetation struggling to grow in the parched ground. They attack the cornfields reducing the stalks to stubs. They then eat their way through the wheat field, oat fields, and pastures crushing the life out of the land, leaving a wasteland behind them. They strip the leaves off the trees, wood from the fence posts, and paint off the buildings.

Marie's hen trips along the dry ground at break-neck speed in hot pursuit of a crusty creature with bulging eyes. She catches a grasshopper in her beak; its ugly legs flailing as she chokes it down. She pursues another and another and even more until she no longer desires what used to be a treat. Having enough, she waddles back to the chicken coop with the look of a child who's eaten too much candy.

"Look what those devils have done to my rug," says Marie in horror while showing Frank her rug riddled with holes. "I just hung it on the line a little while ago, and they've eaten it. I have to watch so they don't crawl in the house and eat my curtains, too."

"There isn't anything they won't try to devour," says Frank as he ties twine around his pant legs to deter grasshoppers from crawling up his legs.

"What's going to happen to us?"

"I don't know, but soon they should have everything eaten and move on. Maybe the worst is behind us."

With the ground laid bare of crops by the devastating hordes and still no rain, the wind whips mercilessly at the dry earth stirring up clouds of dust, carrying for miles, sometimes mixed with red dirt from as far as Kansas and Oklahoma. Day after day of dust storms pile up banks of dirt in the fencerows, over machinery, and up to the roofs of buildings. Driven by the wind, dried Russian thistles break at the root and tumble across the ground coming to rest in the fence line. Prosperity disappears under the dust.

Every living thing suffers from deprivation. In a frantic attempt to save his livestock, Frank harvests the new growth of Russian thistles, the only green plant not consumed by the grasshoppers. Even though the nutritional value of the thistles is questionable, the animals remain alive somehow, although rib and hipbones protrude on the starving beasts.

"We have to do something with the livestock," Franks says to Marie one day. The government will buy some of them for slaughter and will shoot the rest if need be."

"Shoot them?" says Marie incredulously.

"We can't just watch them starve to death," reasons Frank. "My horses can't eat the thistles. It makes them sick. I can't stand to see them suffer. We will have to sell most of the livestock. I don't see any another way."

Marie knows he thinks a lot of his faithful horses. They are like friends to him. With a lump in her throat, she says, "Do what you think is best. You're right. We have no other choice." The day that the government workers come to remove the livestock she purposely remains in the house.

At midday, she strikes a match and lights the kerosene soaked wick in the half empty lamp. Another dark cloud of wind driven dust darkens the sun. Every day repeats itself with the sun rising to a beautiful morning. The wind, at first a breeze, grows in rage until it has unleashed its fury on the land. The house shudders as the wind hurls the dirt against its sides filtering through the windows and doors. Marie wets rags to place at the windowsills to try and stop the powdery dust from entering. In spite of her efforts, the fine powder infiltrates everywhere even in bureau drawers and cupboards. She covers the prepared food on the table and the water bucket with a cloth. Soon the dust settles there too.

Her family approaches the house after harboring the remaining animals in the barn from the rolling dark cloud of suffocating dust. With scarves tied around their faces to protect themselves from the choking dust and the driving grit that cuts against the flesh often causing dirt sores, they rush into the house for shelter.

Her household dwindles in size. Anna has married. Bill and Charley have left looking for work. The rest of the family remain at home, some working for the WPA, the Works Progress Administration, a federal program which provides useful jobs such as dam and road building as well as bridge and building construction. Grateful for having something to eat, no one complains of the simple meal. Marie, not able to raise a garden, uses the last of her home canned vegetables from the cellar. Frank has butchered a beef for meat. No one seems to relish the meal or the conversation.

Towards evening the wind dies down, and the dust storm abates. Everyone leaves the confinement of the house looking somehow out of place and dejected on the barren desert. They can no longer walk through the cornfields, harvest the grain, cut the hay, or water and hoe the garden. There's nothing to do but wait. Many obstacles have stood in their way over the years, but they could always overcome them with determination and hard work. This they cannot beat.

Day after day of heat, dust, and grasshoppers threatens to break the human spirit. Many farmers escape the brown landscape. They pack up what they have left, many in a state of poverty, and flee this hopeless country for somewhere else, perhaps the west coast where it rains. Abandoned buildings stare with hollow eyes across the wasteland.

"I don't know if we will be able to hold onto the place much longer," says Frank one day during breakfast. "We haven't been able to grow a decent crop in several years and what livestock we have left are skin and bone. Land prices are cheap now. I've heard of a place south of here with 160 acres for sale. We could buy it and move there. Son Frank has money put away and has offered to buy it. We would have some place to go."

Marie doesn't say much in response. She has spent thirty years of her life here. She doesn't want to leave and start all over.

The shadow of suffering lessens. Beginning in 1935 a few rains renew hope. Even though Frank does buy the south place, they do not have to move, but the ravaged land has to be rehabilitated. Precious topsoil lies in banks and drifts like black snow. The farmers in the area including Frank implement conservation techniques. First they plant a portion of the over plowed land back into grass. They let other fields remain fallow, to rest for a year, soaking up moisture until they seed it the next year. They also plant alfalfa to restore nitrogen back in the soil; they use fertilizers in the fields, and plant drought resistant forage crops such as milo, sorghum, and cane. They continue to build dams, an expansion of the WPA projects, to catch the runoff from melting snow and rain. The county employs better poison control for grasshoppers.

The 1940's bring more rain draping the earth in a cloak of green velvet. World War II increases the need for agricultural products and boosts prices. Frank and Marie have triumphed over the greatest test of endurance yet.

The Great Depression not only transforms conservation practices but advances mechanization as well. Horsepower can no longer compete with faster tractor-powered machinery. Frank, like many farmers, keeps his team even though the horses plod along in the fields at a top speed of three miles per hour and require oats, hay and rest. He uses his

*Young Frank.*

teams for other jobs on the farm such as stacking hay, corn picking and hauling bundles. Although Frank owns a cumbersome steel wheeled tractor and several pieces of horse drawn machinery, the ability to farm more acreage more efficiently requires new and better machinery especially designed for tractor power. Being conservative and leery of large capital outlay, he makes do with what he has. He hitches up the horse drawn machinery to the tractor requiring an extra person to operate the equipment behind the tractor.

Often Marie finds herself as the extra manpower. During harvest, she rides the binder tripping the lever to release the bundles. Marie dreads coming down the sloped hills. Hanging on for dear life, she forgets to release the bundles. "I hope Frank doesn't notice," she worries.

But sure enough on the next round, Frank shouts back to her over the roar of the tractor, "What happened? Those bundles aren't lined up right."

She acts like she doesn't hear. After all, he should be glad she is trying to help.

Eventually Frank does replace his old tractor for one with rubber tires, a power take off to transfer the power directly from the tractor to the machinery, and hydraulic lifts to raise his machinery out of the ground. He uses money from bene-

*The old cottonwood.*

fit payments received for reducing the size of planted acreage
and also from the rising commodity prices. During the 40's,
he buys machinery especially formulated for the power take
offs, which decreases the manpower once needed.

Because of the exodus during the Dirty 30's, farms decrease in number but increase in size. Farmers who stay, motivated by the ban on acreage restrictions, buy up the deserted farms at reasonable prices. Frank, as well as other farmers, produces as much as he wants to satisfy the war demands and continually adds more land to his holdings.

*Chapter Eleven*

# Fading Journey

Celebrating the return to productive land, the bright green shimmering leaves of a cotton wood tree rustle in the sunshine. Marie shades herself under the outstretched branches of the firmly rooted tree that has witnessed changes over the land. The old tree withstands drought, wind driven storms as well as bright sunshine and plentiful rains. The gnarled branches, a testimony to the passing years, not only endure but also sprout new life each spring in hopeful anticipation of fair weather days.

She watches dusty cattle trail in from the southeast toward the corrals and large barn that Frank built earlier, one of the largest in the area, to facilitate care of his cattle. Over the past few years Frank and his sons begin to rebuild their herd, practically wiped out during the depression. He raises white-faced Herefords, a breed of cattle brought over from England in the 1870's to upgrade and eventually replace the lanky longhorns and Shorthorns of earlier years. When wintered properly, the Herefords do well on the plains and produce marketable stock. Frank usually sells his grass fed two-year-old steers to market in Sioux City, Iowa.

Twenty years have elapsed since the collapse of the surrounding cattle empires in the land of the Rosebud. The stock market crash, drought, disease, and the encroaching farmer have hastened their demise. Frank, as well as surrounding farmers, begins to combine ranch economics with farm economics, realizing the grass naturally supports herds of cattle. Like other ranchers, Frank brands his cattle, a common practice to provide evidence of ownership that dates back to Biblical times.

Frank, now a rancher as well as a farmer, heats his irons in a fire until red-hot. Marie, curious of the branding procedure, observes as the men separate the bawling cows from the calves. After the chaos of sorting, the brothers run the calves into the chute where they apply three hot irons searing the brand B/F onto the hide that burn through the stench of smoking hair. Marie moves to be upwind from the cloud of smoldering haze.

"Marie, check the stock tank so it's not running over," hollers Frank above the din of bellowing cattle.

Marie walks the short distance from the corrals to the windmill. Its creaking metal blades turn in the stiff breeze rhythmically pumping gushing water into a waiting stock tank. She picks up a bucket, skims aside the green globs of scummy moss on the surface of the water, and places it under the pipe to catch the flowing water. She waits awhile before she pulls the rope folding the vane that applies the brake to stop the turning action of the windmill, and then she picks up her filled bucket. She approaches a small building that is home to the new guineas she previously set from eggs and pours water into their pan. The squawking commotion of the watchful fowl warns her of a rattlesnake, still prevalent on the place. Her mongrel of a dog jumps into action seizing the coiled snake with his ferocious teeth before she has time to search for a weapon. After a lengthy struggle the snake, still writhing, lies dead.

"Good dog," she says to him and then gives him a pat hoping that he did not get bitten in the attack.

Later that fall when the heat of the day lessens its grip, Frank stops in the house carrying a watermelon grown by a neighbor living on one of the islands down on the river. "I have a treat for us, Marie, thanks to a good friend. We'll have a slice, and then I'm going to the Grim place. Want to come along?"

"Sure, what are you going to do there?" she asks.

"Grim has his land up for sale, and I want to look it over once more. The 280 acres will fit in with our land quite nicely if we decide to buy it. I'll give you a driving lesson on the way over," he offers. He teases Marie about driving lessons every time he brings home a new car, this being their third.

"There's no way I'm going to drive your clattering contraption. Besides I have you and plenty of sons and daughters to drive me around," she says while splitting the melon with a sharp knife releasing the sweet juices of the perfectly ripe fruit. After savoring their cooling treat, she cleans up the table. "I'll be right with you, but first I want to put on a clean apron."

Frank slides onto the seat under the car's steering wheel. As soon as Marie tidies up, he motors them along the road eventually turning off onto a trail that winds itself down into a wooded hollow isolated from the plain above. Sumacs along the trail drop reddening leaves, splashing the ground with crimson. Trees and thickets fill the ravines with their glowing fall colors. The feel of dampness held by the shaded underbrush and seasons of decaying leaves arouse a distinctive fall aroma. Drying creek beds shrivel into irregular squares of curling mud waiting for the days of melting snow where once again the little creatures and plants of the watery world will reappear.

A sod house unobtrusively appears secluded against a hill partially hidden by trees and brush. The Grim family still occupies the modest structure and has expanded its usefulness by building additions and a roof of wood. A spring trickles down the side of a rocky incline not far from a root cave dug in the side of a bank.

Deer crash through the thickets and brush as Frank and Marie ascend a steep portion of the road. Prairie chickens fade into the browns and tans of the season. The Chevy groans as it climbs out of the microcosm of tranquility.

After a short distance, Frank stops the car, and they get out to look over the lay of the land. The breeze blows graying wisps of Marie's hair as they amble up to the top of a hill.

"The land is a little rough, but there's good shelter for the cattle, some pasture land, and farm ground up here on the top," says Frank.

No longer belly deep to a horse, the native grasses yield to fields that interlock into a patchwork of stubble left from the harvest, fallow land, maturing corn, the bronzing, beaded heads of milo, and pastures speckled with contented grazing cattle. "I wish we could stop time for awhile. Just think what more we could accomplish," reflects Frank as he surveys the evidence of their toil.

"We aren't that old yet. There's plenty more we can do," Marie says as she gently links her arm through his.

*House on the Grim place in the late 1950s.*

During the winter months that follow, Marie notices that Frank doesn't tackle his everyday chores with the gusto he use to have, and he seems to rest more now. Not wanting to be coddled, he shuns her pleas to see a doctor. But finally after several months, he realizes something is wrong and agrees to go. A trip to the local physician arouses suspicions of a serious illness resulting in a referral to the Mayo Clinic in Rochester. Marie accompanies Frank for the week stay. They rent a place provided for the patients and their families where she can cook their meals and watch over him.

After all the tests have been concluded and the diagnosis made, they pack up and leave Rochester for home. Their worst fears have been confirmed. The usual spirited conversation between them lags on the seemingly endless trip back. How do they tell the family that Frank has cancer and probably doesn't have long to live?

Usually so observant of each minute change in the landscape, Frank doesn't comment on the greening pastures and grain fields as they drive up the lane into the yard. Marie stiffly eases out of the car. It's been too long of a trip for one day, but Frank wanted to get back to the place as soon as possible. She can't blame him, though. She helps unload the packages and suitcases from the car and tucks a sack of seed potatoes that she bought in Minnesota under her arm. She intends to get these into the ground tomorrow.

"Something smells good in here," says Frank trying to sound cheerful as he enters the house.

"We're trying out a new recipe, Dad. It's called vegetable meatloaf," says Agnes, setting a couple more places at the table.

Young Frank climbs down the stepladder with a bucket of water and rag in his hand. "What are you doing there?" Marie asks motioning toward the scrub pail.

"I know how you like to get your spring cleaning done before planting time, so I thought I would help you out and wash down the walls," he says.

No one speaks a word about what the parents found out in Rochester. The look on Frank's face says it all. Vincent, Agnes, daughter Marie, young Frank, and Charley sit up to the supper table, and then Frank and Marie tell them.

Day by day, Frank's cancer worsens, and he is hospitalized. On July 11th, he gives up the battle with a disease not well understood at the time.

With each swing of the pendulum on the living room's regulator clock, time moves forward. Several weeks have passed since Frank's death. Tall trees close in around the house, their leafy forms casting shadows across the floral wallpaper. Marie sinks down in a wide armchair in the living room with a deep sigh and studies the family portraits on the wall. A flood of memories rushes back to her as her eyes rest on each picture. Her mother, such a strong support in her life, has been gone for twenty-seven years now. Her large family, grown into young men and women, are about to venture out on their own. For some time her gaze lingers on her wedding portrait. "We were so young and had such dreams," she utters to herself. Talking to Frank seated so still in the picture, she continues. "For forty years we battled this stubborn land, made a living, raised a family, and settled a place that drove many away. We did all right. In spite of all the hardships, we found our dream."

She rises and walks to the door looking out over the time-less landscape standing so steadfast and unaffected by change. Reflecting on the stillness of the hills, she wonders if they know that the one who has loved them and worked so hard to care for them will no longer look to the east for a promise of a new day.

Marie, now alone, looks to the misty river hills in the early morning sun. But she continues the dreams she and Frank once shared with her sons, daughters, and their descendants.

She leaves the house for the potato patch picking up her hoe hooked on a branch of the contorted cedar tree she insisted that Frank help her plant years ago. She calls to her dog, a faithful companion, who eagerly runs to her side and lifts his head for a quick stroke. Out of habit she checks the sky for rain. "*Prset,*" she mutters under her breath. The nagging wind tugs at her clothes. Tying her scarf tightly under her chin, she leans into the gale.

Seated: Agnes, Frank, Marie and Anna. Middle: Emil, Frank, Marie, Vincent and William. Back: Ed and Charley.

Vaclav, Barbara and family. Photo courtesy of Bob Brozik

*Rosie (Frank's sister). Photo courtesy of Karen Bailey*

*Frank and Marie's farm. Photo courtesy of Bertha Brozik*

Marie with two of her granddaughters, Barbara (Bill's daughter) and Deb (young Frank's daughter).

Marie's granddaughter, Janice, in Marie's living room with her mother Bessie and father, young Frank.

# Recipes

Even kolaches take hard work. Czech Proverb

# Kolaches

1½ cups water
1½ cups milk
½ cup instant potatoes
1⅓ sticks oleo
¾ cup sugar
2½ t. salt
3 eggs
2 pkg. yeast
10 cups flour

- Dissolve yeast in warm water and let stand five minutes. Scald milk and let cool. Add yeast mixture, sugar, oleo, and salt. Stir in instant potatoes; add eggs and enough flour to make a soft dough. Put in greased pan and let rise to double. Pinch off enough dough to make balls the size of a walnut. Let rise until soft. Make a deep depression with fingers in the center of each ball. Fill with poppy seed, apricot, prune, or any desired filling. Let rise a few minutes. Bake at 400º for 15 minutes.

## Prune filling:

- Cook 2 lbs. prunes. Cool. Pit and chop very fine. Sweeten with 1 1/2 cup sugar. Add a pinch of salt, 1/4 t. each of cinnamon, cloves, allspice, 1 t. lemon juice and 2 T. melted butter. Mix well.

# Potato Dumplings

2 cups mashed potatoes
½ t. salt
1½ cups flour, more may be needed if too sticky
2 eggs

- Mix and roll out on a floured board into a thick rope.
- Cut the roll into pieces of dough the size of a walnut, shape each piece like a potato.
- Drop in hard boiling water for five to seven minutes. Cover with lid.
- Serve with sauerkraut and melted butter.

# Houska

• Scald 1-cup milk and then add ½ cup sugar, ¼ cup butter, and 2 t. salt. Let cool to lukewarm. Then add 1-cup flour. Soften 2 packages yeast in ¼ cup lukewarm water. Add to first mixture. Mix in 1 t. grated lemon rind, ¼ t. mace, 2 eggs, ½ cups white raisins, and ½ cup blanched almonds. Add about 4½ cups flour, gradually, to make soft dough. Knead on a lightly floured board until smooth, cover, and let rise until doubled. Punch down and divide into 5 equal parts and let rest 10 minutes. Roll each portion into a long strand, place 3 strands on a greased baking sheet, and braid loosely beginning in the middle. Twist the remaining 2 strands and place on top of other braid. Tuck the ends under and seal well, cover, and let rise until light. Bake at 350° for about 40 minutes. Frost and decorate when cooled.

# Fruit Dumplings

  2 cups flour
  2 eggs
  2 t. baking powder (not level)
  ½ t. salt
  ½ cup milk

- Mix dry ingredients together.
- Make a well in the middle of dry ingredients, and then add beaten eggs and milk.
- Knead till dough is smooth, use as little flour as possible.
- Pinch off a piece of dough.
- If using Italian prunes, dip prunes in boiling water until they soften unless they are very ripe. Do not let crack while in the boiling water. Purple plums can be used also.
- Wrap pieces of dough around fruit.
- Drop into boiling water for 8 to 10 minutes.
- Boil 5 minutes uncovered and then cover for the remainder of the time.
- Split tops after cooked to let steam out.
- Serve with melted butter, cream, cinnamon and sugar.
- Makes six dumplings.

# Sweet and Sour Cabbage

- In a skillet, melt 2 T. butter.
- Add chopped onion and sauté.
- Add chopped cabbage and sauté a while longer.
- Add a little water, cover and cook until transparent.
- Add 2 T. vinegar, 1 T. sugar, salt and pepper.
- Sprinkle 1 T. flour over cabbage.
- Add a little more water if needed.

# Crackling Bread

2 cups flour
½ t. salt
3 handfuls of fine cracklings
Milk

- Work flour, salt, and cracklings together by hand. Add enough milk to hold ingredients together into dough. Divide and roll out into rounds to desired thickness. Bake on cookie sheet at 375°. Flip the rounds once until browned.

# Oatmeal Cookies

*(Unfortunately, this isn't Marie's original recipe, but it is close to it)*

1 cup of cooked old fashioned oatmeal, cooled
½ cup lard or shortening
1 cup white sugar
1 large egg
1 t. vanilla
1½ cup flour or more if needed
1 rounded t. baking powder
¼ scant t. soda
½ t. salt
1 t. cinnamon
1 cup raisins

- Cream the lard, brown sugar, and white sugar together. Add egg, cooked oatmeal, and vanilla. Mix thoroughly. Add the dry ingredients. Mix well. Add raisins. Drop a tablespoonful on cookie sheets. Bake 350° for ten to twelve minutes.

# Lye Soap

- Pour 11 pints of rainwater into a crock or enamel pan.
- Add 1 box borax and stir.
- Then add 9 pints of melted lard, be sure it's cool but melted.
- Add 2 cans lye.
- Stir 25 minutes, no longer.
- Pour mixture into pans and cover with a heavy rug.
- In the morning, cut the soap into bars.
- The mixture is thin, but it will thicken when it hardens.

# Marie's Mustard Plaster

    1 tablespoon powdered mustard
    3 tablespoons flour

- Mix with about half water and vinegar to make a stiff but not to dry dough. Put in cloth and sew up so it can't run out. When it gets cold, reheat in any pan.